HEALTHY HOME

HEALTHY

JILL BLAKE

HOME

*A practical and resourceful
guide to making your own home
fit for body, mind and spirit*

David & Charles

A DAVID & CHARLES BOOK

First published in the UK in 1998 by
David & Charles

Design copyright © The Ivy Press Limited 1998

A catalogue record for this book is available from the British Library.

ISBN 0 7153 0839 4

This book was conceived, designed, and produced by
THE IVY PRESS LIMITED

Art director: Terry Jeavons
Designer: Alan Osbahr
Commissioning Editor: Viv Croot
Edited by: Ann Kramer
Page layout: Alan Osbahr and Siân Keogh
Picture research: Arlene Bridgewater
Three-dimensional models: David Donkin, Mark Jamieson
Illustrations: Jerry Fowler, Lorraine Harrison
Feng shui consultant: Jane Butler-Biggs
Architectural research: Dominic Bailey

Printed in Hong Kong

CONTENTS

I have always believed homes should be planned for happy living and that, because no two families have an identical lifestyle, requirements, or the same budget, every home will be a highly individual unit, planned, designed and decorated to suit those who are going to live in it. This drive to individuality can be seen clearly in a row of terraced houses, all built to the same design. As soon as new owners move into one of the houses, it takes on an entirely different look from the house next door, both inside and out, as the new owners plan rooms, choose colour schemes, select furniture and furnishings, and plant the garden to suit themselves. 'Nest building' is the current buzzword used to describe this phenomenon – I prefer to call it creative homemaking.

For at least 100 years there has been plenty of help and advice available for would-be homemakers from the publication of august tomes such as Mrs Beeton's Book of Household Management through to the more recent proliferation of specialist and non-specialist magazines and supplements, to say nothing of television programmes all devoted to different aspects of interior design, decoration, furnishings and garden planning.

Today there is much more to the art, science and craft of homemaking than in previous decades.

PREFACE

We want our homes to be attractive and possibly stylish, as well as being happy places. We also want them to be healthy. We are aware of the problems of pollutants that can enter our homes either from the materials used to build and furnish our homes, or that can creep in from outside. We want to make our homes more environmentally friendly, to run them without making a drain on energy and other resources and without using materials that will damage our wider environment. The current interest in the ancient philosophy of feng shui also reflects our concern to create a healthy and harmonious home environment.

Interest in alternative energy, practical insulation, recycling and organic gardening is widespread and has already affected governments, builders, developers, architects, manufacturers and retailers, as well as homemakers. Fortunately, therefore, we are in a good position to use environmentally friendly products for the home.

But health is not only about being environmentally aware, it is also about creating a healthy atmosphere. In this book I have tried to help you to create a healthier home by suggesting ways of planning, designing, decorating and furnishing, as well as fitting everything into the available space, that will suit your particular lifestyle and which

will be sympathetic not only to the environment but also to the original architectural style of your home. I have also recommended user-friendly materials, healthy housekeeping, maintenance and cleaning, as well as giving some advice on how to heal existing problems.

While researching this book I have gained an even greater respect for the way our grandmothers and great grandmothers ran their homes efficiently and economically with very little in the way of appliances. Many of the things they did were not only practical but also thrifty – and healthy; they certainly knew about recycling, and we could well take a leaf out of their books.

I hope you will enjoy reading *Healthy Home* and that it will help you create as healthy and happy an environment as possible, in which you and your family can live with pleasure, where you can shut the door on the outside world, relax, be stimulated, follow various hobbies and pursuits and above all, improve the quality of your life.

JILL BLAKE

BEGINNINGS

The function of a home is to provide shelter but approaches and styles have varied through time and place, often moving interior and exterior design well beyond basic needs. This elegant Nash terrace, for instance, reflected the wealth of its original occupants.

Towards the end of the 19th century, the Art Nouveau movement rejected the harshness of industrialism in favour of natural materials and craft-based furniture and furnishings. Flowing lines reflected forms found in nature.

WHERE DID IT ALL BEGIN: the enthusiasm for design, decoration, colour and style expressed in the desire we all have to create our own special environment?

Initially homes provided a basic shelter from the elements, although maybe even then there were attempts to stamp the inhabitant's personality onto the fabric. But, by and large, it was only the rich and aristocratic who were able to have their houses and castles architecturally designed and the interiors styled to personal taste, including carpets and furniture. In fact, in some cases, the designer even provided an accurate plan stipulating the exact positioning of furniture and artefacts, all of which had to be replaced exactly by household staff after accommodating guests, or cleaning. Homes such as these were designed to impress royalty or nobility; they were rarely comfortable or homely!

Beginning in the 18th century, the Industrial Revolution brought

enormous changes, not least in the ways in which buildings and their contents were constructed. The then emerging middle-classes, with newly found wealth, made a cult of the home, and began to build smaller and often spectacular houses. The Nash Terraces in London and the flamboyant Royal Pavilion in Brighton paved the way for an increasing interest in design and architecture, so that an elegantly designed house, both inside and out, became the aspiration of all but the most impoverished.

But interior design, as we understand it today, did not really come into fashion until the inter-war period, when contemporary decorators such as Elsie de Wolfe, Sybil Colefax, Syrie Maugham and Eileen Gray became fashionable and the rich and famous commissioned them to design the interiors of their houses.

At much the same time there was a vogue for Modernism, or the International style, which was based on functional, minimalist design, advocated by architects such as Walter Gropius, who founded the Bauhaus school in 1919, Mies van der Rohe, Le Corbusier and Marcel Breur, who believed in applying the principles of industrial design to the interior – rejecting the past completely. Interestingly, this approach and style is now re-emerging with the popularity of 'lofts' – large open-plan interiors, which are often constructed in disused warehouses or factories.

Interior design and decoration – and of course building – was put

Modernism embraced industrial processes and moved design away from the natural environment to a starkness reflected in the current emphasis on minimalism, which reduces the home environment to its most bare elements.

under wraps during 1939-45 war, and for some time afterwards. Shortage of materials meant that it was only possible to build fairly simple or functional houses. Now this has changed dramatically – in Britain, for example, change began with the 1951 Festival of Britain, which claimed to promote the best of British design – and interior design has become a fashion industry, with as many new trends appearing and disappearing almost as fast as in the clothing industry.

ECO-DESIGN These days much is written, discussed and televised on the need to design and build 'green' homes. This began during the 1960s and 1970s with the greater awareness of the need to conserve energy. Alternative energy centres, such as the Centre for Alternative Technology in Machynlleth in Wales, appeared and 'show' houses were displayed at exhibitions or built on exemplary sites.

Initially the main concerns were conservation – of energy, water and other resources – and the use of sustainable building materials. But although many of us may not yet have got round to the most basic energy conservation in our own homes, we have moved on from this stage and there is now a growing movement among architects, industrial and interior designers, garden designers and even builders and manufacturers to consider the wider ecological aspects of the buildings they create and the materials and products they use.

True ecological design looks at the home and other buildings in relation to the wider environment. Ecological design is concerned with saving or replanting trees and other native plants; preserving streams, lakes, wetlands and local landscape, perhaps building sympathetically around them; and reducing pollution in the construction process. The height and width of buildings too are planned so that they are not starkly aggressive or dwarf the landscape, perhaps screened with existing trees, rocks, hillsides or other natural features, or with the landscape redesigned round them.

Ecological designers have also reassessed vernacular design, using colour, form, materials and also structural traditions that are native to the particular area, often using local brick, stone and clay and even indigenous soil. In this way, they create a building which is truly at home in its environment. As a result of this trend, many traditional and natural building products have been reintroduced, such as timber frames, many of which may well be recycled, clay blocks, lime mortar and plaster. Even earth and grass are used as building materials and some of the buildings themselves may be partly buried in the landscape.

This approach to building design is becoming increasingly important and there are various associations and organizations which you can join if you are planning to build or convert to a more environmentally friendly home. Recently too, in Germany and Scandinavia, a movement has emerged devoted to 'building biology', or *Baubiologie,* which combines the scientific and ecological approach with a holistic view of the relationship between buildings and people so that buildings too are seen as living organisms.

Recent years have seen an increasingly strong movement towards ecologically influenced design that emphasizes the need for homes to harmonize with the natural environment both in style and fabric.

THE PERFECT ENVIRONMENT

DEFINING A HEALTHY HOME

As daily life becomes increasingly pressurized, there is unprecedented interest in nest-building, creating homes that meet deep needs. But despite pressure from television and magazine features, creating a healthy home need not be expensive.

TODAY, we can barely pick up a magazine, switch on the television, or browse through a book shop, without realizing that tremendous pressure is being put on all of us to create the perfect environment, one which expresses our personality and at the same time is stylish, stunning, environmentally friendly – and effortless. And many of these magazine features and television features suggest that it is both inexpensive and very easy to carry out an effective 'make-over', whether of just one room, your entire house or your garden.

Of course, what you don't actually see is the army of helpers who carry out the decorating, produce those stunning soft furnishings, re-upholster the furniture, lay spectacular floorings, hang pictures, and position tasteful accessories such as cushions or wall hangings. Nor is the cost ever mentioned. What you are most likely to see are so-called interior designers discussing the current trends and trying to impose their taste and will on the viewer and the reader – and in doing so often promoting the latest, and quite possibly short-lived, styles and ideas.

But creating a healthy and happy home is not just about following design trends unthinkingly. It is also about meeting personal needs, about creating the right space for you. Professional interior designers will not impose their will on their clients; they will be at great pains to ferret out the needs, requirements, likes and dislikes of all of those who will be living in the house.

So what constitutes a healthy, happy and harmonious home – apart from one which is light and spacious, welcoming, practically planned, attractively decorated and furnished, filled with natural and user-friendly materials, and surrounded by a verdant garden?

A really happy and healthy home has an indefinable quality; you can sense good 'vibes' the moment you enter the front door, sometimes even as you walk up the front path. This instinctive reaction cannot be explained by builders, property developers, estate agents or house 'doctors', a growing band of people who ferret out the history of your house or advise on improving it to make it more saleable. It is a hard feeling to pin down but it is certainly one that we need, so much so that many would-be purchasers today

call on feng shui consultants to advise on the most favourable aspects of their property and whether it will be good for the health and luck of the occupants.

A truly healthy home is a place which is good for you and your family not only physically but also mentally, emotionally and spiritually. It should be somewhere pleasurable to return to in the evening, somewhere where you can relax, shrug off the worries and tensions of the day and be yourself, a place that contains some personal space where you can shut the door occasionally on the rest of the world. It should be a creative environment, where you can indulge in cooking, gardening, sewing and other hobbies and somewhere that is comfortable enough to enable you to flop with your feet up, watch television,

listen to music, read, play a musical instrument, pursue a craft, in short to do whatever it is that you want to do without feelings of tension or anxiety.

Your home should also have an invigorating ambience; it should be a pleasure to wake in the morning in surroundings that you have created yourself, perhaps surrounded by a colour which suggests sunshine even on the coldest, bleakest and greyest of days. Your home environment should inspire, stimulate, calm and, above all be a source of great enjoyment both to yourself and others who enter it.

Finally, a healthy home should be non-polluting both for your health and that of the wider environment. It should be safe, free from toxins and as full as possible of natural and user-friendly materials.

A healthy home has an almost indefinable quality – it just feels right. More tangibly, it should be light, airy, comfortable, welcoming and non-polluting. Above all, your home should be somewhere that enhances your physical and mental wellbeing.

11

TAKING STOCK

Don't rush into changing your home. The first step towards creating a healthy home is to get a feel of the space you live in. Change nothing for a year or, if you prefer, paint everything white so that you can observe how changing light and seasons affect your home.

BEGINNINGS ARE always difficult, and creating a healthy home takes time; it can't be done overnight, no matter how easy a televised make-over appears. Most of us won't be working with professional designers; we will be doing our own design and decoration, and in the welter of advice on offer, it is often hard to know where to start and what to choose.

Possibly the very best advice is to start by doing nothing, except spending time getting a feel for and understanding of your surroundings. This is not always easy, especially if you have lived in your property for some time. Try to

forget all the existing colour schemes, decorations and furnishings and imagine that you have a clean 'canvas'. Try to remember how you felt when you first saw the inside of your home; if you can't remember, get a friend or family member to jog your memory.

And if you have just moved, or are about to, don't rush to change anything. Until you have lived in your home for at least a year, experiencing each of the changing seasons, you will not know how your various rooms feel in spring, summer, autumn or winter and how the natural light affects them as the seasons pass. If you really

> **"Have nothing in your house which you know not to be useful – or believe to be beautiful"**
>
> (WILLIAM MORRIS)

Traditional Shaker homes made good and thrifty use of materials to hand. Their approach to homemaking was practical. They created space by hanging chairs on walls but this may well have been prompted by an intense work ethic as well as tidiness.

can't live with the existing decor, just paint everything white or some other fairly neutral colour; live with bare floorboards and simple blinds at the windows while you get an awareness of how you want your home to be.

Apply this same rule to patios, conservatories and gardens. Wait to see what is already present and what growing things will emerge during the spring and summer and how their arrival changes light and shade inside the home and out.

BEAUTY AND FUNCTION
Once you have a feel for your home, you can then get to work. Really successful design is about the fusion of the practical with the aesthetic – surfaces, materials, furniture and all the components of an interior

should be chosen to suit the purpose and function of the area in which they will be used as well as reflecting the particular lifestyle of those who will be living there. And it is these considerations that will dictate the choice and colour of rooms, the texture and wearability of fabrics and how all surfaces are treated. And, of course, consideration must be paid to the original architectural style in which the building was constructed.

Good design and the resulting functional, comfortable and healthy home is the result of careful planning and working to one grand master plan. To achieve a good and sympathetic environment, you need to plan your home and the spaces within carefully and the first section of this book gives you detailed advice that will be helpful.

But you need more than clever, functional planning: you also need to think about budget and just how much money you have available. Creating a healthy home need not be expensive; you will probably have to work with existing structural constraints and may find that you can incorporate many existing items. Words such as salvage, recycling and thrift can take on whole new meanings as you make use of what already exists to create your healthy home. In fact, many things now associated with tradition began as the practical use of materials which were to hand. The patchwork quilt, for instance, was a way of using up old scraps of fabric. In the United States this craft has become an art form. In Shaker communities, old metal was used to create lamps and boxes.

USING
FENG SHUI

As WELL AS USING conventional interior design, many people today are increasingly interested in using feng shui to achieve a healthy and harmonious home. Put simply, feng shui is an ancient art of placement, based on the idea that the way you organize your home, choose rooms, decorate them and place your furniture can enhance wellbeing. Some of the principles are different from interior design but there are also many parallels.

Feng shui is not new although it has only recently arrived in the West. It is an ancient Chinese philosophy, with origins that date back at least 5,000 years. Translated literally, feng shui means 'wind and water' and its main aim is to achieve balance and harmony with the natural environment by arranging or altering your surroundings according to certain principles. Applied to the home, or to offices and other buildings, feng shui can be used to enhance the happiness, prosperity and good fortune of the occupants, while creating serene, healthy and balanced surroundings.

FORM AND
COMPASS
There are many different schools of feng shui, some of which have been adapted for modern use. The oldest is the Form school, which places emphasis on the importance of natural landscapes – hills, mountains, rivers and other land forms – for enhancing wellbeing and evaluating the quality of a location. Gradually this evolved into the Compass school, which introduced the idea that specific points of the compass exert

unique influences on different aspects of life. South, for instance, with its orientation towards the sun's heat, has a more extrovert and energizing effect than the colder, more introverted north. Today, feng shui practitioners use blends of the different schools according to need or circumstance.

CHI
Feng shui is based on the belief that there is an invisible life force or energy known as chi that circulates both within ourselves and throughout the universe. In order to live well and healthily, we need to harness this force and encourage a healthy flow of chi energy into our homes and lives. Feng shui practitioners would argue that if our lives are stagnant or if we are depressed or lacking

in energy, it is because this fundamental chi energy has itself become blocked, negative or unhealthy not necessarily because the spaces within them are cluttered, poorly organized or destructive in some way.

A key concept in feng shui is that everything in the universe is made up of two opposing but complementary energies – yin and yang. Yin, for instance, is dark, yang is light. Health and wellbeing come when our homes reflect a balance between the two.

FIVE
ELEMENTS
Another important concept is that of the five elements or energies: fire, metal, wood, water and earth. According to feng shui these are the basic elements of the

Good feng shui aims to balance yin and yang. The green plants, harmonizing colours and the play of light and shade in this sitting area (left) produce a healthy balance, although the sharp-cornered plinth could disrupt energy. Clear spaces and use of curves in the kitchen (right) promote smooth flowing chi; red flowers boost fire energy.

YIN	YANG
Shade	*Light*
Female	*Male*
Passive	*Active*
Moon	*Sun*
Earth	*Sky*
Soft	*Firm*
Water	*Fire*
Winter	*Summer*
Cold	*Heat*

Just as some people call in professional interior designers, so too it is possible to call in a professional feng shui consultant.

A consultant will:
■ look at a property, ask details of your birth place, date and time and draw up a horoscope to establish whether you and your new home will be compatible;
■ possibly check on previous occupants to establish how their health, wealth and happiness progressed while they were living there and will advise on whether you are likely to enjoy the same prosperity, or bad luck. What suits one person may not, of course, be right for another.
■ produce a written or verbal report on the feng shui of the property, including details of the chi energy flowing in and around the building and whether or not you will prosper in your potential new surroundings
■ report on the changes you may need to make to improve the feng shui of the building. If these are fairly minimal, the consultant may recommend buying the property; if they are too difficult or costly or if the home is unsuitable for you, the consultant may suggest that you find an alternative
■ a feng shui consultant will also advise on your existing home and, if there are problems, will suggest simple remedies.

universe and each of us is born into one of them. Together they create an unending cycle that can be either creative or destructive. Each of the elements is also associated with a particular compass direction, colour and various other attributes, so that by introducing one or more of these into the home you can boost, enhance or activate one of the energies according to your personal needs, so improving your life situation.

Professional feng shui practitioners spend many years perfecting their art and some of the principles behind feng shui are quite complex. But feng shui is also all about encouraging us to return to a more intuitive approach to placement so if you find that your home feels good and if you feel well in it,

then you have probably, though unwittingly, followed good feng shui practice.

Much of feng shui practice, like sensible interior design, is based on common sense. A room that is uncluttered, for instance, obviously has an ambience that encourages uncluttered thought. We can do very little about where our homes are located but we can do a great deal about how we organize our living spaces inside our homes and feng shui principles can be incorporated quite simply by changing the use of a room, rearranging furniture, using certain colours, balancing light and shade or simply by adding plants, mirrors or other objects to boost or activate healthy energy flows into and through the living spaces of the home.

SETTING PRIORITIES

For relaxed living your home must match your lifestyle. This minimalist style with its white walls, natural wood floorings and varying levels is streamlined, beautifully designed and easy to maintain. It would be good for adults but unsuitable for children.

THERE ARE MANY STYLES that you can choose for your home. The building itself may influence your final choice but ultimately style must also relate to and reflect your personal lifestyle. A streamlined, minimalist interior, totally devoid of clutter and with lots of light, wide open-planned space and vast glazed windows, furnished with the bare essentials, may well suit a single person or childless couple. But this style is rarely compatible with toddlers and small children, and may well be unsafe for them. So the arrival of children may mean moving into a more conventional living space or making structural changes. Flexibility has to be an essential ingredient when styling and planning your home.

Age and lifestage will be influential. Those in their 20s or 30s, who lead a busy life, may prefer a fairly streamlined minimalist interior, which is easy to clean and maintain and perhaps with no garden to tend. If children arrive, you may want to change properties and add a garden. If you are in your middle years, with an active family, you may prefer a more cosy lifestyle, and may need a two- or even four-bedroomed house with more than one bathroom, a living and dining room, surrounded by a good size garden with the potential for creating several different outdoor spaces – somewhere for children to play, somewhere to enjoy *al fresco* meals and perhaps a vegetable and fruit garden. As further changes occur, you may even consider changing the use of various rooms in the house according to changing needs.

You may either choose to move home several times to accommodate life changes, or to adapt the same property in many different ways over the years. Moving can be highly stressful and, like planning a house, needs to be planned as carefully as possible in order for such a big change to run smoothly.

THE NEED FOR PLANNING
Whatever stage you are at, you will want to be able to live as comfortably as possible in your home, so it needs to be well planned with plenty of storage space to accommodate the

For most families the arrival of children alters the definition of a healthy home and changes priorities. In this home, small tables might need to be moved, but the hard-wearing surfaces and materials, level floors and access to the garden are all ideal.

clutter of family living. To achieve harmony, you will need to plan your space so that you can move about and perform various tasks relatively effortlessly; you will also need different rooms for different activities: sitting, relaxing, sleeping and cooking. Style will play a part in planning, but so too should comfort and efficiency.

USING COLOUR

You can get a great deal of enjoyment from deciding on design, playing with patterns and choosing colour schemes. Colour is an important part of any healthy home because the colours you select will play a major role in creating mood and ambience; they can stimulate or relax, provide warmth or cool down a space. The type of patterns you use, your

furniture, curtains and blinds, will all help to create or 'set' a distinctive style as well as creating an appropriate atmosphere.

Colour and style are discussed more fully later in the book but when you are working with a whole house or flat, don't forget the importance of whole house colour co-ordination.

If you live in a fairly small house or apartment, aim to carry colour on from one room into another; this way the whole area will feel more spacious and create a sense of continuity. The hall, stair and landing area in particular, which should be warm and welcoming, should relate to all the areas or rooms leading off. Floor colour can provide this link; either by using the same floor colour throughout (it need not be all the

Colour sets atmosphere and mood. Vibrant yellow walls and a red carpet make a welcoming hallway. Moving the yellow up the stairs provides a link with the rest of the house and a feeling of continuity.

same material or texture) or by using a patterned multicoloured flooring in the hall and on the stairs and then separating out the individual colours to use singly in different rooms.

Whole house scheming does not mean that a whole home has to be decorated in similar colours; this could be extremely boring. But aim to work with a similar colour palette: choose several colours for the main surface, but ring changes from area to area, introducing some interestingly coloured accessories, which are easy to change and which will help to define the function and style of the space. You can work mainly with neutrals, with warm or cool colours, and bring in sharp contrast by using accessories.

You can also use colour to enhance good features in your home, play down less attractive ones and improve the proportions of different rooms. Colour can also lighten dark areas; warm cool spaces; and create feelings of intimacy or space.

LIGHT, SENSUALITY AND NATURE Planning a

healthy home also means making the best use of light, both natural and artificial. Aim to encourage as much natural light into your home as possible, and then use artificial lighting to enhance dark areas, ensure safety, and provide well-lit working areas.

Making links with nature also brings harmony and health into the home. In order to make your home healthier and pleasant aim to create indoor green spaces in your living areas, even more so if you have no garden. It is surprising what you can do with house plants, herbs and flowers; they brighten the home and improve the air quality. Outdoor green spaces too, whether garden, patio or balcony, provide pleasurable and relaxing additions to every home.

A healthy home should also be sensual and calm. Scents, pleasing sounds and water features enhance every environment; fabrics can muffle intrusive sounds and are also a pleasure to touch and live with. A quiet home, free from unwanted sounds, is good for health, constructive family life and for times of meditation.

WORKING WITH NATURAL PRODUCTS Whatever the

decisions you reach on planning, colour and furnishing, aim to use as many natural materials as possible. They are healthier and more pleasant and enjoyable to live with; they are also likely to be more tactile than synthetic fabrics and artificial materials.

A healthy home is non-polluting. We know now that many products such as lead-based paint or asbestos, once used in many homes as an insulator and fire barrier, actually present serious health hazards. We are still using plastics and foam for upholstery, now known to be a serious fire hazard that gives off dangerous fumes if it does catch fire. We also use laminates and MDF (medium-density fibreboard) for built-in furniture and kitchen units, and vinyl floor and wall coverings, all of which give off formaldehyde. Many homes also contain synthetic fabrics as well as dangerous adhesives and glues and highly caustic substances for stripping off old paint. All these should be replaced with more user-friendly products, even if this does mean there will be a little more work and elbow grease involved.

It is far better to furnish and decorate using natural materials such as wood from fast-growing deciduous trees like pine or recycled timbers; fabrics such as linens, cotton and wool; and wood, cork, linoleum or rubber for flooring; or recycled quarry tiles, flagstones and earthenware *carres* instead of vinyl.

Furnish and decorate your home with natural materials: cane, woods, rushes and organic paints. Avoid using synthetic materials and other harmful, toxic or polluting substances such as formaldehyde or vinyl.

Introducing natural
sounds and scents
from the garden,
living with the smell
of cut flowers and
encouraging daylight
into the house are
very simple ways of
enriching your home
and making links
with nature.

Book-filled shelves
are practical but also
create an interesting
archway, while a
polished wooden
floor links the two
areas. The result is
a calm, peaceful and
ordered living space.

POINTS TO CONSIDER

Buying a home is one of the most stressful life decisions. Plan it carefully and make a list of your needs before deciding. A town home gives access to shops, transport and other services; a home in the country brings you closer to nature but may mean dependence on a car.

IF LIFE WERE PERFECT, we might well elect to design and build our own homes by employing an architect, builder and interior designer to realize our ideas on an attractive plot of land with services such as electricity, gas and main drainage nearby. And of course it would need to be conveniently situated for work, schools, shopping, leisure activities, and socializing – difficult if not almost impossible to find in most areas of our overcrowded world.

If you are embarking on designing and building your own home, try and plan from the inside out. List all your requirements but maintain a flexible approach. Think ahead and plan for what may be very different needs in five, 10 or even 20 years' time. This will mean planning the interior so that certain spaces are flexible and

multipurpose and walls will be easy to move or alter. The practical Japanese system of sliding schogi is an interesting idea, although perhaps not one that many of us would use.

If you are starting from scratch you will also be able to consider incorporating environmental and health aspects by installing energy-saving devices such as solar heating, adequate insulation, double- or triple-glazing and water recycling, asking your architect to build your home around your definitive list, subject to financial considerations.

Alternatively, you may opt for a form of prefabricated building; either modern or older barn or timber-framed building, which can be moved from one site to another and adapted to suit your needs.

Most of us have to choose a property which is already built and has had previous occupants. You may choose a period property, or something more modern. Always think about your requirements before making a final decision.

You will first need to decide where you want to live: town, city, suburbia or countryside. Rural sites are often considered ideal for bringing up young children or for retirement. But think carefully before making this decision. Shops, schools, medical services may be at some distance and you will need to check out the efficiency of public transport, if you do not own a car, or if you are concerned about the environmental implications of car ownership.

If you opt for a city or town location, check the proximity of parks and other green sites as well as local schools, shops and public transport. In some large cities, these can be as scarce as in the countryside. Also consider the problems of air and noise pollution. If you are buying a flat, check access, including lifts and parking facilities. You may find a home in a leafy suburb will provide you with a good compromise.

Once you have decided on location and the size and type of property, contact local estate agents in the area of your choice and also read the advertisements in local newspapers. Be as precise and definitive with an estate agent as you would be with an architect if you are building your own home; don't waste time making appointments to view unsuitable ones.

When you do go to view, keep an open mind. Don't be put off by other peoples' decorations, furniture, furnishings and carpets. Imagine the rooms as if they were empty and undecorated, a blank slate on which you will create your own home. Look carefully at the fabric and state of the structure and also check how much natural daylight the rooms receive. Think too about orientation – the way in which rooms face. Determine which rooms receive early morning sun, ideal for bathrooms and kitchens, and which receive the afternoon sun, good for sitting rooms or dining rooms. It is important to consider which way the garden or patio faces: a north or north-east facing garden will be cold and dark in the afternoon. Also be aware of overshadowing

buildings or tall trees; not only will they shade your property, tree roots can also damage the foundations. If you are buying a flat, you may also want to establish discreetly who your neighbours are.

But in the final analysis it is up to you to choose a home which has the right vibes, where you and your family will be happy, which will suit your needs, requirements and lifestyle, and which has the potential to be designed and decorated to your personal tastes, whether it be a modern, functional loft space, or an older style home.

FENG SHUI SITES

If you are a devotee of feng shui you may well decide to call in a feng shui consultant who will see whether the house is suitable for you and your family, examine its location and orientation and look at whether there are adverse environmental factors such as pollution. Other points that he or she will consider will include the health and happiness of the current occupants.

In feng shui an ideal site should also enable the building to be backed by a hill or mountain because beneficial chi will flow into the building and detrimental, chi will be deflected away – in the absence of hills or mountains, tall trees or even high buildings could be substituted, but they should not be too close or they will cut natural light; tall buildings can also be obtrusive and invade privacy. There should be water nearby – possibly a river, stream, lake or bay in front of the site.

Wooden beams, simple furniture and all-day light make this a truly natural home. Barn conversions such as this are increasingly popular but are only suitable for those with the time, energy and finances to invest.

For good feng shui, your home should be backed by hills, on a gentle slope facing slow-moving water. Such sites can be hard to find. An alternative might be this peaceful house, standing in its own space, sheltered by trees that are not oppressively close.

CREATING A

HARMONIOUS HOME

SPACE AND

HARMONY

The starting off point for a harmonious home has to be the building itself – and the spaces or rooms within it. Each room is a basic shell, which you can plan, design, decorate and furnish to suit your needs. Your home is the place in which you live, work, relax, eat, store possessions and socialize; the way you plan your space will reflect all these activities. But a really healthy and harmonious home should also be a happy one, where family members can relax and enjoy their surroundings and not be afraid of making a mess!

Balance and harmony are essential both to health and good interior design and are often the result of combining the practical and the aesthetic. Your space has to be designed to work for those who will use it. But it also needs to be a pleasant, healthy and attractive environment, one that enhances physical and spiritual wellbeing. Think too about change or time passing. Plan wisely and use your space creatively. Your home is not static; during the course of its lifetime it will have to adapt to changing needs as the family grows up, or family members become elderly.

Within the house, you need to consider the purpose and function of each room, choosing flooring, wall decoration, fabrics and furniture as appropriate. Rooms that have to withstand the rough and tumble of family life will need easy-to-clean elements and hard-wearing floorings. Keep fragile fabrics and delicate hand-printed wallpaper for less active, more restful areas.

Safety and hygiene too are important points to consider, particularly in bathrooms and kitchens. Don't forget halls and stairways in your planning either – these are the entrances into your home. They need to be warm and welcoming, hinting of good things to come in the rooms beyond.

After working out the practicalities, you can think about colour for mood and atmosphere, form to create interest and movement, pattern to set style and texture to add an extra visual and tactile dimension.

Using space harmoniously also means considering the basic design style of your property. You should plan and decorate with sympathy for the original architectural intention, restoring and renovating any interesting original features. Emphasize attractive details such as lovely fireplaces, decorative cornices and ceiling mouldings, arches, rustic beams, original window frames and internal shutters by the clever use of colour, pattern, mirrors and lighting. Use subtle decorating techniques to 'fade' unattractive features into the background.

But avoid the temptation to over-improve. Modest houses and apartments look best decorated and furnished simply in minimalist style, both inside and out. Harmony is also about environmental sensitivity. Don't stone clad or colour beautiful mellow bricks, or add windows, pillars, porticoes, porches or other features that are out of keeping with your home's façade or those of neighbouring properties.

WHOLE HOUSE PLANNING

ESTABLISHING REQUIREMENTS

A family's demands on their home change with time. For example, as the children grow up and leave, space can be adapted or redesigned. Perhaps a bedroom that is no longer needed could become a home office.

BEFORE YOU BEGIN to plan the spaces in your home, sit down and analyse what you have – determine the purpose and function of each room, work out exactly what you want from the space. Ask yourself how it will be used, and by how many people at a time. What do you want those rooms to be? In professional design terms, this is called 'taking the brief' and often involves using a pre-prepared questionnaire to establish likes and dislikes, needs and requirements and any restrictions, such as budget, time scale, the need for planning permission, which might need to be taken into account. You too can work a list of questions, and involve the rest of the family in making decisions.

THINKING ABOUT THE WHOLE HOUSE
It is often best to consider the whole house first. There is no need to be conventional about allocating rooms to particular locations. Bedrooms, for example, do not necessarily have to be upstairs, or sitting and living rooms on the ground floor.

Be flexible in your thinking. Consider using downstairs rooms for dining, family rooms and a playroom. Upstairs, the main bedroom could also be used as an adult's only sitting room. And if your home is becoming too small for a growing family, and moving is impractical, you may think about extending and enlarging the your home, although planning an extra space needs careful thought. An

Plan carefully for your home's future needs – today's nursery may become a toddler's playroom or teenager's bedroom.

attic conversion may not be wise for noisy teenagers, nor is it practical for elderly relatives. Instead, an attic conversion might be ideal for a study or office, an adult's bedroom, or a sitting room – especially if there are fantastic views.

If your house has an integral garage, you could convert it into a work or hobbies room, or a playroom. It could become a practical study-cum-office, maybe with separate access, or even a dining room, allowing your existing living room to become a more luxurious sitting room.

Ultimately you will make the choices that are most appropriate for you – influenced often by light, space, positioning, and the feel that you get from individual rooms.

EASY FLOW
Planning rooms too needs thought and analysis. You need to consider the basic characteristics of each room – its size, shape and orientation, the way it faces. You also need to think about how much natural daylight it receives, as well as the actual state of the fabric.

Aim to create a comfortable 'traffic flow' in each room, avoiding awkward obstructions, providing good storage space, and creating an environment that is positive and workable according to the purpose and function of the room. When planning, think about how doors and windows open, and where to place chairs, beds, sofas, and other furniture so that they do not obstruct flow through the room.

MULTI-FUNCTIONAL ROOMS
In today's homes, with restricted space, you may need to plan some rooms to be multifunctional, or split-functional as they are more usually known in feng shui. This can be harder than planning a single-purpose room. You will need to be flexible, especially when choosing furniture, storage and surfaces in order to make sure that they will suit the different activities taking place.

One room, for instance, may have to be both spare bedroom and home office. Think about a sofa bed, which will provide both seating and sleeping facilities. You will need office storage, but also something that can incorporate clothes for an overnight guest. A desk too may have to serve as a dressing table. Floor, wall and window treatments will have to be more practical than in a conventional bedroom.

THINK AHEAD
Planning space also involves thinking ahead. What begins now as a nursery may, over the years, have to evolve into a bed-sitting room for a teenager. Your kitchen may now only contain basic items; in the future you may be adding more equipment as your needs change.

KNOCKING DOWN WALLS
Think carefully before knocking down interior walls and creating a vast open-plan space – this may be a wonderful design feature for a loft, where the essential look is of one large multipurpose area, but do consider your own lifestyle, how much privacy you want. In an open-plan area everything will be on permanent view.

THE ANCIENT ART OF PLACEMENT

The setting sun relaxes energy levels, making a west-facing room calm and peaceful. Touches of red boost fire energy and prevent stagnation.

INTERIOR DESIGN uses the practical planning of space, suitable storage and decoration to create harmony in the home. Feng shui too places great emphasis on harmony and efficiency but also on organizing space to ensure a healthy flow of energy and to encourage, boost or stimulate various aspects of your life and personal needs. Some thinking can be complex and those who want to organize their homes strictly according to feng shui principles sometimes call in professional consultants to advise them.

In feng shui the type and siting of a property, as well as its surroundings, are extremely important and can have positive or negative effects on energy flow and on the occupants of the house. Some principles may at first sight seem contradictory, but with consideration they can also make a great deal of sense. For instance, a small house in a cul-de-sac may appear to epitomize calm and tranquillity; a feng shui practitioner, however, might argue that such a situation could block energy flows, leading to stagnation.

Orientation too, the direction in which a home or room faces, is also of great significance, particularly in the Compass School of feng shui, which believes that specific points of the compass exert profound influences that should be

Sunlight activates or boosts energy so choose rooms accordingly. An east-facing room, for instance, makes a good kitchen. Healthy plants encourage wellbeing.

Ancient luo pan compass

considered when planning space. South, for instance, represents heat, midsummer or midday so that any south-facing room boosts energy, and should be used for that purpose. A south-facing room for instance would make a good playroom or a place for midday parties. By contrast, north is a colder direction, encouraging inwardness and quiet contemplation. A north-facing room might therefore make an ideal study or a library. East is the direction of the rising sun, bringing morning or rising energy; such a direction might be good for a kitchen where the energy can be cooked into the food, or a breakfast room or child's bedroom. West is the direction of the setting sun, and where energy flows relax; use west-facing rooms for relaxation, perhaps to create a peaceful sitting room for calm family or social gatherings of friends .

BOOSTING LIFE CHANCES

According to feng shui, different areas of your home relate to particular aspects of your life, namely: wealth; fame; relationships; ancestors; health; children; knowledge; career; and benefactors. By organizing your space with these in mind, either by allocating rooms to particular areas of the house, or by organizing the space within individual rooms themselves, you can boost or influence these different aspects of your life. Balance and harmony always remain the ultimate aims of feng shui, so that, when planning space, you should aim to keep these aspects of your life in balance.

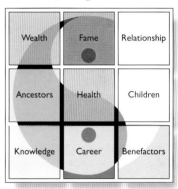

Nine areas of the bagua

In feng shui there are nine important life aspects, which can be related to different areas of the home. Health comes when these aspects are in balance.

Feng shui practitioners might argue that a cul-de-sac is not a good place to live because it traps energy, causing stagnation. Others might see a cul-de-sac as a calm haven.

Divided into the nine principal life aspects, a bagua 'template' (above) can be placed over a plan of your home showing how the aspects and areas relate. Working from this, you can organize your home to influence your life chances. The template is always laid with the front door in the knowledge, career or benefactor area (far left).

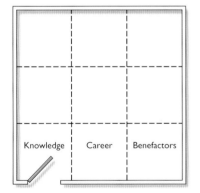

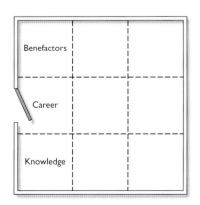

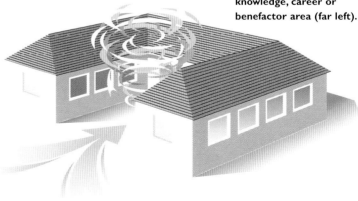

TAKING MEASUREMENTS

CREATING A HARMONIOUS space requires careful planning. Once you have decided on the purpose and function of your rooms, and know what you are going to want in the way of furniture, storage and so on, you need to produce floor plans to scale. With these you can plan your use of space in a practical and efficient way.

As well as making a floor plan, you can also produce a wall plan, known as an elevation. This is essentially a flat plan, which also shows the accurate positioning of doors, windows, fireplaces, radiators, skirtings, picture rails and so on. Even though the plan is not shown in perspective, you can use it to plan three-dimensionally, deciding how to treat windows, built-in features such as shelves or wardrobes, and even where you are going to site wall lights.

Your plan will be invaluable. You can take it with you when you are buying furniture, or choosing materials for any colour schemes.

You can use it to plot the position of so-called services – plumbing, lighting, telephone wires – so that they harmonize with their surroundings and your furniture, and to decide on any structural work, which should obviously be done before decorating.

Measuring up

To measure up accurately you will need: a good steel tape (fabric ones stretch in use) – preferably a 5 or 7m length retractable tape; a plumb line so you can measure vertically; and a spirit level to find the true horizontal. You will also need scrap paper, a pencil, and possibly a calculator. A willing partner to hold the other end of the tape and double-check your calculations can also be an asset. You may also need a stepladder and torch.

Gather together all the equipment you will need to make a master plan before you begin to organize your home; the process will prevent mistakes later.

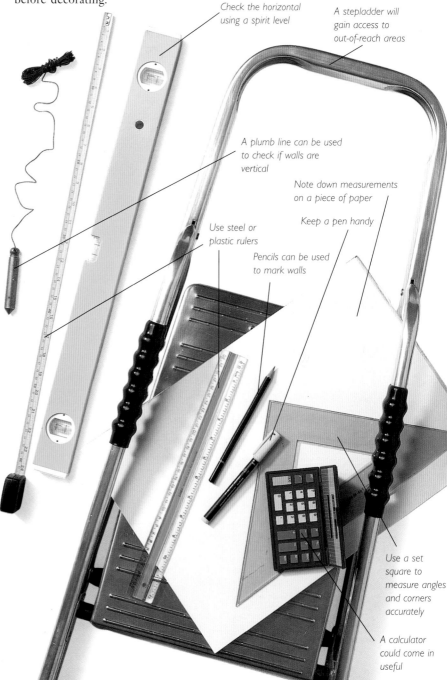

Check the horizontal using a spirit level

A stepladder will gain access to out-of-reach areas

A plumb line can be used to check if walls are vertical

Note down measurements on a piece of paper

Keep a pen handy

Use steel or plastic rulers

Pencils can be used to mark walls

Use a set square to measure angles and corners accurately

A calculator could come in useful

MAKING THE
PLAN Make a quick sketch of the room on plain paper. Follow the shape of the room, including recesses and projections such as chimney breasts. Indicate doors, and which way they open, as well as windows, radiators, fitted furniture or fixed appliances such as baths or cookers. Include pipes, electric points, and light fittings.

Measure everything accurately, and jot figures on the sketch plan. Start measuring in one corner of the room, and work round systematically until you are back where you began. Keep the tape taut, and always measure on the true horizontal and vertical, using your spirit level and plumb line to check the accuracy.

Think three-dimensionally and measure the width and height of the walls, taking your measurements at several different places because they are rarely perfectly square. Measure diagonally from corner to corner across each wall as an extra check.

Once you have accurate measurements, translate them onto a scale floor plan and wall elevations, by drawing up accurate plans on the squared paper. Indicate the

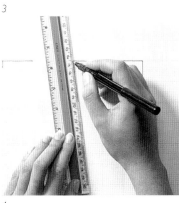

Make a plan by first drawing a sketch (1). Then take accurate measurements, noting these on the sketch before drawing up a plan on squared paper (2). Trace the plan onto plain paper and make overlays for lighting before inking in and tracing off the final plan (3 and 4).

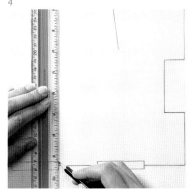

thicknesses of walls, show how windows are inset, and which way they open. Include the thicknesses of doors. Use a set square to achieve perfect angles, and a compass to indicate curves such as door swings.

Choose a scale to suit yourself and the size of the room – the usual scale is 1:20, 1:25, 1:50, or 1:100 – the plan, therefore, will be 20, 25, 50 or 100 times smaller than the actual floor or wall – and all measurements should be reduced to the same scale. It also makes sense to draw floor plans and wall elevations in similar scale, so they relate to each other.

Finally, trace your plan off the squared paper onto plain paper. You can then make tracing-paper overlays for any lighting plans or window treatments and lay them over the master plan.

Once you are happy that the plan is neat and accurate, ink in the lines firmly, so you can see them clearly through the tracing paper, then trace off the complete plan. Don't forget to indicate the scale on the plan, and compass orientation. Do not write measurements on a scale plan, as this defeats the object of the exercise. You can photocopy the tracing-paper drawing, using it like a negative, if you want a more robust plan – and extra copies.

FITTING
IN THE
FURNITURE

YOU CAN USE your floor plan to decide how to position your furniture and appliances, such as bathroom or kitchen equipment. Measure each piece of furniture carefully, whether it is already in your home, or when you go to buy it. Then, working to the same scale as your plan, cut out the shapes on squared paper or solid card to make templates, and move them about your floor plan.

Remember to allow enough room to open windows, drawers, and doors. Bear in mind the space that you need for moving furniture,

perhaps when making beds or cleaning, or for pushing chairs back from desks and tables. Plan to use space in such a way that people can move easily through and around the room, without being hampered by awkwardly positioned pieces of furniture. Take particular care with some multi-purpose items such as sofa beds, desks with drop-down flaps, and folding tables. Measure and template them carefully, open and closed, to see how much space they take up in both positions.

When positioning furniture, you should always aim for a feeling

Pieces of coloured paper, cut to size as furniture templates, can be moved and positioned on your floor plan.

Flowing curtains at the windows or above a bed add a touch of intimacy and warmth, softening a square room.

of harmony. Avoid 'confrontational' situations when you open the door to a room. Don't place a sofa in such a way that the door bangs the arm or back; it disrupts energy and causes irritation. Feng shui practitioners also advise against placing chair backs facing doors, as this too disrupts the flow of energy into and around a room. Beds and lavatories should not be visible.

Avoid placing desks and other work surfaces in dark corners facing the wall; instead place them under a window, at an angle, or facing forward into the room. In this way, you will be looking into the room, rather than literally feeling hemmed into a corner. You are aiming always for a smooth movement of energy and traffic flow through the room.

Once you are certain that everything is placed well, and that you can use the room with ease and comfort, use your templates to trace the shapes and positions of your furniture onto your plan. In this way too you will be able to make sure that lighting, plumbing and other services fit into the room harmoniously. This type of planning is particularly useful if you are moving house, but it is also a good way of planning existing space. It is much easier to work with small pieces of paper and card, than to heave furniture about.

PLANNING AN EXTRA VISUAL DIMENSION

Designing a room is not just about fitting in furniture, it also involves considering the forms or shapes that will sur-

round you, and that can provide an extra visual dimension in their own right.

Contrasting forms – ovals, circles and curves – combined with square and oblong forms will appear to change the shape and perspective of a room. A curved seating arrangement, for instance, will bring a feeling of harmony and interest into a squarish room; an L-shaped arrangement of furniture can divide a long, thin area, and create a split-purpose room. In the dining room, an oval or circular dining table will complement a long, slim sideboard or storage units. In the bedroom, a circular bed can add interest and offset the rigid lines of built-in wardrobes. Such forms add extra visual interest to any shape of room.

You need not confine contrast to the horizontal plane; think three-dimensionally as well, varying the heights of furniture as well as their shapes. In high-ceilinged rooms you can use different items of furniture to offset the height, but in low-ceilinged rooms avoid tall pieces of furniture. In a kitchen or dining room you could combine a dresser with a simple refectory-style table, or a circular one. In the bedroom, an unusually shaped headboard will add extra interest to the bedhead wall, or you could use some interesting drapes above the bed, but avoid any sense of hemming yourself in. To add interest too, place a circular or oval mirror above a square fireplace or, to provide contrast, between two long, slim sash windows.

A tall, dramatic, four-poster bed sets off a high-ceilinged room to perfection, while the round mirror above the square fireplace adds contrast.

Well-planned furniture placement allows for easy, flowing movement through and around a room.

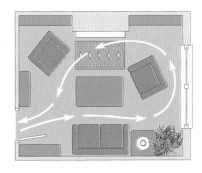

33

SPACE AND HARMONY

STREAMLINING YOUR HOME

IN BOTH FENG SHUI AND INTE-RIOR DESIGN, a healthy approach to space involves avoiding clutter. We all acquire possessions; they are an integral part of our lives. But too much clutter and disorder can bring not only specific health hazards, but also tension, anxiety and depression, a sense of not being able to cope. According to feng shui too, excess clutter disrupts the flow of energy, causing stagnation and tiredness; sorting your possessions and clearing out clutter from time to time can have a very refreshing effect.

At the same time, however, the things we own have practical uses, and are often objects of beauty. Creating harmony therefore involves good storage, and using available space creatively. From a practical point of view, it makes sense to store items you use frequently in the areas where you use them. China, cutlery, linen, glasses and so on need to be stored close to the dining table for example, perhaps in a sideboard, units or a cupboard. Clothes, shoes, handbags and accessories are best stored in the bedroom, but overcoats, hefty boots and sports equipment may be best kept close to the front or back door.

STORAGE SOLUTIONS

Closed purpose-designed storage such as wardrobes, chests, or drawer units often provide ideal storage solutions. You can put possessions away neatly, but also have quick access to things you need. Some decorative items too can be displayed on open shelves, as an integral part of your decorative house schemes.

Some homes, however, have limited space for fitted or free-standing furniture. If this is the case, look at your home again. There may be many places where you can install suitable storage, which you have not yet considered. A window seat, for example, with a lift-up top can be used to store things like magazines, newspapers, games. Or you can store clothes or toys in drawers under the bed.

Think about building shelves in unusual places – tailored to fit into the wall at the side of a bay window for example, or to each side of a sash window. None of these solutions will take up much floorspace, yet the overall effect will be sleek and streamlined.

USING SPACE CREATIVELY

Most homes contain usable space if you look for it – both overhead and underfoot. It may be practical to board over the joists in the loft, install a glazed roof light and electricity, and use this space for storing items which are not used every day, or to make full use of a cellar. Remember, however, to check and reassess the contents regularly. But there is no reason to tuck away frequently used items. Ceiling racks, for instance, once used in kitchens to air clothes and dry herbs, can be used either for their original purpose, or to support tools, sports equipment, or clean towels in the bathroom. They can also be used for hanging baskets, or attractive kitchen pots and pans.

Working in a similar style, think about wall-mounting the traditional wooden plate draining rack for storing plates, cups and saucers.

There is often usable space above a door or window, where you can site a cupboard, or you may be able to add extra shelves inside existing wall-mounted cupboards for storing infrequently used items such as Christmas decorations, picnic baskets and so on. And, if there are picture rails in your house, you could install a wider shelf above them to display, or store, attractive china and porcelain. Another popular, and traditional method of storage, is the Shaker-style peg rack – a wall-mounted rail complete with projecting pegs that hold a variety of objects – clothes, fabric bags filled with items – even dining chairs!

A cheap and easy way of removing clutter from rooms is to screw simple hooks to the edge of

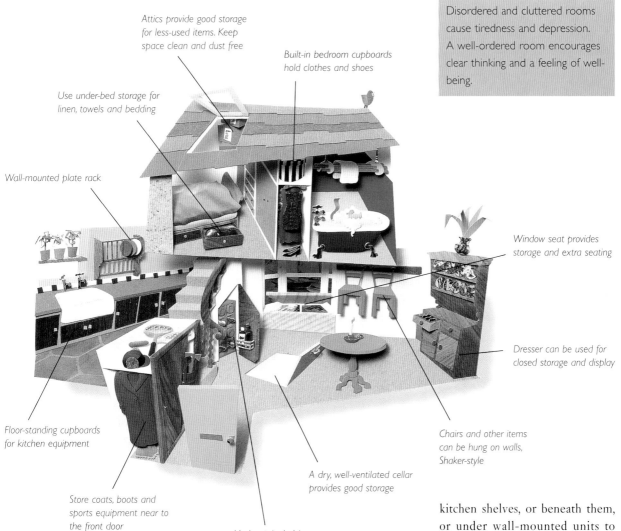

Attics provide good storage for less-used items. Keep space clean and dust free

Built-in bedroom cupboards hold clothes and shoes

Use under-bed storage for linen, towels and bedding

Disordered and cluttered rooms cause tiredness and depression. A well-ordered room encourages clear thinking and a feeling of well-being.

Wall-mounted plate rack

Window seat provides storage and extra seating

Dresser can be used for closed storage and display

Floor-standing cupboards for kitchen equipment

Chairs and other items can be hung on walls, Shaker-style

Store coats, boots and sports equipment near to the front door

A dry, well-ventilated cellar provides good storage

Under-stair shelving or cupboards

Home should be an escape from the chaos of daily life so use all potential storage space to remove clutter and create a relaxed environment.

Be creative. Possessions don't have to be tucked away in dark corners. Suspend pots and pans from a ceiling rack and hang your summer hats, Shaker-style, from a pegged trellis (far left).

Constant tidying up is exhausting. Wicker baskets stacked into open wooden shelving (left) can provide a simple and healthy solution for vegetables and fruit.

kitchen shelves, or beneath them, or under wall-mounted units to hold cups, jugs and other items with a handle. They can also be used in garden sheds, or in a child's room for hanging toys.

Other places too can be adapted for storage. The area under the stairs can be shelved and used for storing wine racks, bottles and tools. The backs of built-in cupboard doors can be fitted with hanging hooks, racks or plastic containers. This type of arrangement works well in the kitchen, where tinned and dry goods need cool, dark storage. Make sure doors and hinges are strong enough to take the extra weight. If necessary cut existing shelves into an elongated U-shape to accommodate storage on the back of the door. If cupboards are deep, install a light which comes on as the door is opened.

Simple, adjustable shelving can hold a variety of possessions.

PLANNING FROM THE INSIDE OUT

YOU CAN PROVIDE instant storage in many different ways: free-standing pieces, flexible adjustable shelving, and built-in storage, which you can build yourself or brief a professional carpenter. But before you go hunting for storage, work out exactly what you want to store, as well as its size and weight, and then fit storage to needs. In an ideal world, storage would be planned from the inside out so that you organize it around what you need to store.

Measure everything you want to store – its height, weight and density – and relate your measurements to the width, depth, height of existing drawers, shelves, wardrobes and cupboards. In the bedroom, for example, consider how much space your clothes need, hanging or folded, as well as considering other items that might be kept in the room such as luggage, handbags, accessories and so on.

With dining area storage you will need to check the dimensions of serving dishes and stacks of plates, the space needed for glassware, bottles and decanters. Storage requirements in the living room may be very extensive; you may need to find homes for a variety of possessions from books and glasses to CDs, music system and television. Books in particular come in a multitude of sizes and can be very heavy. Adjustable shelving is often the most practical solution, supported on brackets that fit into a special slotted angle screwed to the wall. Such shelving can be used on its own in recesses, or combined with units, chests or cupboards to create 'closed storage' or built-in units for large items such as a television or hi-fi system.

Glass shelving too works very well and can be used in living rooms, bedrooms and bathrooms. It is functional and can be very decorative, particularly if well lit to highlight possessions that you want to display as well as store.

INSTANT STORAGE

Today there is an enormous range of instant storage available – much of which is extremely attractive, providing a stylish as well as a practical solution to the question of clutter. You can use clear plastic containers for clothes, shoes, linens and small accessories; metal and wire minimalist-style items which look particularly good in hi-tech kitchens, or home offices; wicker and cane pieces which have an attractive rustic look; colourful plastic stacking storage boxes. These are ideal for playrooms or a teenage bedroom and can even encourage tidy habits.

Instant storage also includes folding cupboard containers and boxes for filing systems; portable stacking racks; fabric containers for items such as jewellery; tie-up laundry and linen storage, and decorative 'tents' to disguise clothes-hanging spaces.

Display shelves such as glass or wicker containers can be used decoratively to display colourful and interesting items such as pulses and pastas in the kitchen, attractive soaps and creams in the bathroom, or costume jewellery in the

Almost any container from a filing box to a wire basket can provide an instant storage solution and be attractive in its own right.

bedroom. Baskets too can be attractive and easily portable containers. Simple hooks, peg racks and pegboards together with their displayed items also provide interesting visual features.

If you need 'closed' storage to keep out dust and dirt, consider linen baskets and boxes in the bedroom and bathroom, adapt tool boxes or make use of purpose-made needlework and hobbies

baskets. Old luggage, cabin trunks, sturdy ottomans with lift-up tops, wicker hampers and large theatrical skips, hold an enormous amount and are interesting objects.

But before you rush out to buy the enormous choices on offer, do check that your preferred storage solutions will actually meet your needs, both in terms of storing goods, and fitting into the style and space available.

Fabric shelves, hanging from a pole, are colourful and space-saving, but not always practical if overloaded. Before spending money on storage, check it meets your needs.

A custom-designed wardrobe can answer your specific storage needs. Build one yourself or hire a professional carpenter.

Drawers and shelves can be fitted under and around hanging racks. Shoes can be stored under dresses and coats

Remember the extras — weekend bags and sports equipment, for example — and plan extra shelves. They are sure to be filled in no time!

CREATING AN ENTRANCE

Your hallway is one of the most important areas in the house. It is usually the point of entry into the home, so it should be welcoming and have impact. It is also the connecting area to all other rooms, and needs to be planned so that the transition to other rooms is easy and harmonious. You need good access and ease of movement through to the other rooms; consider using colour or pattern to make visual links between the hall and rooms beyond. If you have a tall, narrow hallway, think about using mirrors and colour or pattern to improve the proportions from a visual perspective.

Plan for the number of doors in the hallway, particularly considering which way they open. Make sure there is good air circulation – you may need to rehang a door to make circulation easier – but avoid draughts. A screen or closed porch can help to prevent them.

Most halls are not rooms in their own right, so plan storage carefully in this area to avoid clutter. Create a specific place for letters, keys, clothes brushes and so on; likewise somewhere practical and ordered for outdoor clothes. A telephone might be sited in the hall, so try and organize somewhere to sit comfortably plus a shelf or table where you can write messages, and somewhere to store telephone directories. A hall mirror will add dimension and light, as well as enabling you to check on your own appearance before leaving the house.

In feng shui a red door brings luck into the home. Entrances and hallways are often neglected, but, as the way into your home, they should be bright, warm and welcoming, for you as for others.

FENG SHUI HALLWAYS

In feng shui the entrance to the house has enormous importance, as it is here that both people and energy enter the home. Your front door should be bright, well maintained, and welcoming. It should not be too large in relation to the hall, otherwise energy escapes, something that can be counteracted by hanging wind chimes at the entrance. Flowering or green shrubs in the porch or on the front doorstep are attractive and also encourage wellbeing. If your hallway or corridors are small, narrow or dark, hang a mirror on one wall to give a sense of greater width, and to boost energy flow. If your hallway runs directly through to a back door, feng shui practitioners believe that energy will rush directly through and out of the house; a mirror placed at the end of the hallway can prevent this from happening. Landings should be light and airy, and furniture and storage kept to a minimum.

Health point
Make sure hallway and stairs are well lit and free from draughts

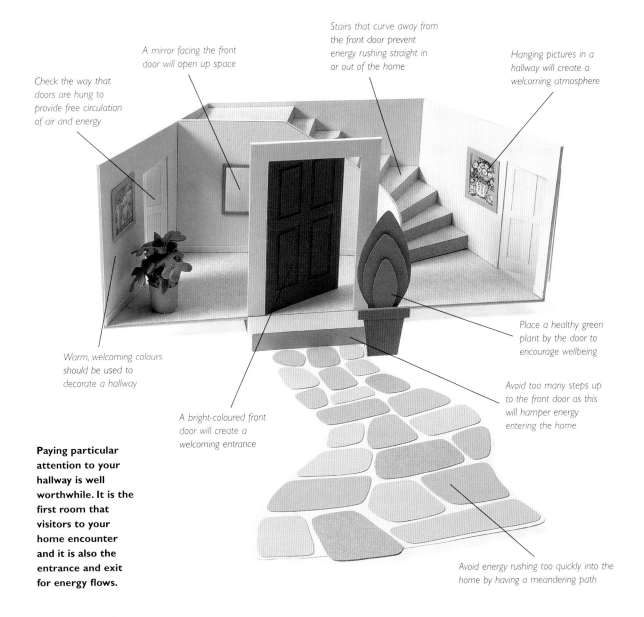

A mirror facing the front door will open up space

Stairs that curve away from the front door prevent energy rushing straight in or out of the home

Hanging pictures in a hallway will create a welcoming atmosphere

Check the way that doors are hung to provide free circulation of air and energy

Place a healthy green plant by the door to encourage wellbeing

Warm, welcoming colours should be used to decorate a hallway

Avoid too many steps up to the front door as this will hamper energy entering the home

A bright-coloured front door will create a welcoming entrance

Paying particular attention to your hallway is well worthwhile. It is the first room that visitors to your home encounter and it is also the entrance and exit for energy flows.

Avoid energy rushing too quickly into the home by having a meandering path

LIVING SPACES
THE DINING ROOM

Eating and drinking are important. This traditional dining room has a sumptuous feel conducive to a dinner-party atmosphere. Candles on an oval table encourage socializing, while red-coloured walls create warmth and stimulate appetite.

By contrast, this modern living space, which contains both dining and sitting room, is much calmer. Pale walls, skylights and a total absence of clutter combine to produce a simple, light and spacious environment for everyday meals and small gatherings.

Dining chairs should be comfortable so that diners remain seated at the table for longer to enjoy their meal.

A DINING ROOM might be the hub of the home – a separate room from the kitchen, and the place where family meals and entertaining take place, with good wine, food and conversation. If this is the case, plan to create a cosy, intimate ambience, as well as looking at the practicalities needed for serving hot food and drinks.

The room should contain a table large enough for family and guests. Round tables encourage a more harmonious eating and socializing environment where no one person feels excluded at one corner or another, so consider this in your planning, perhaps choosing one which extends to an oval. Folding or extending tables are useful when space is limited. Choose comfortable chairs, that relate well to the height of the table, allowing people to be seated without hitting knees or elbows. Think carefully too about the amount of space needed to push chairs easily back from the table without knocking into other items.

If space allows, create a separate space for serving food. This should be sited as close to the door as possible, or under a hatchway to the kitchen. A portable trolley is a practical alternative when space is short.

Plan storage for all the items you need for serving, eating and drinking. If the room is a split-function room, possibly doubling as a dining room and study, use a screen, bead curtain or something similar to divide the room into two areas, one for each function.

FENG SHUI DINING ROOMS

For feng shui practitioners, as for anyone else, eating is an important activity, so the dining room should be planned with this in mind. The aim is to create a harmonious and good feeling among the diners.

Furniture should be kept to a minimum – perhaps only a dining table, chairs and sideboard. Here too oval or circular dining tables are recommended because they nurture harmony and balance, both within the room and among the diners. The shape supports the energy flow and has what is known as a 'gathering' influence; rectangular tables are best kept for more controlled situations such as business meetings. Natural wood is recommended for both tables and other surfaces.

Ideally eating and food preparation should be separated, so that the dining room and kitchen are apart from each other. If this is not the case, you can create a separation using a room divider or perhaps a bead curtain.

Mirrors can be used to good advantage in the dining room – by reflecting food and diners they effectively increase abundance and wellbeing, as well as stimulating energy flow, which in turn stimulates conversation.

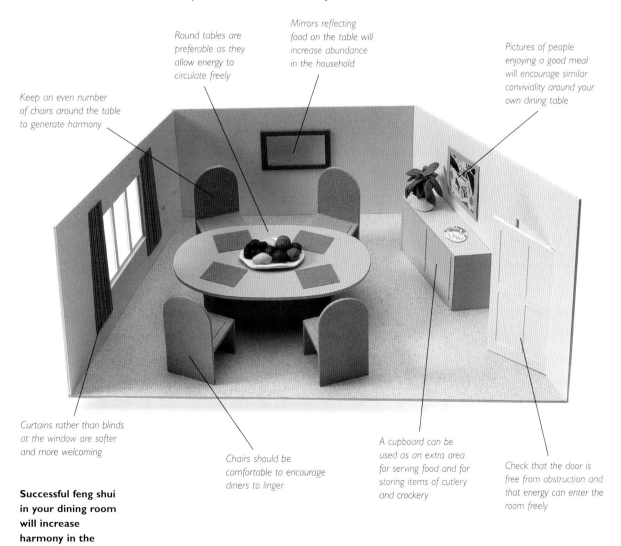

Round tables are preferable as they allow energy to circulate freely

Mirrors reflecting food on the table will increase abundance in the household

Pictures of people enjoying a good meal will encourage similar conviviality around your own dining table

Keep an even number of chairs around the table to generate harmony

Curtains rather than blinds at the window are softer and more welcoming

Chairs should be comfortable to encourage diners to linger

A cupboard can be used as an extra area for serving food and for storing items of cutlery and crockery

Check that the door is free from obstruction and that energy can enter the room freely

Successful feng shui in your dining room will increase harmony in the home and lead to convivial gatherings.

LIVING
SPACES
THE
SITTING
ROOM

THESE DAYS a formal drawing room is very rare; instead, sitting rooms are more likely to be used for family living. Also appropriately known as living rooms, they need to be versatile because so many activities are likely to take place. You need therefore to plan carefully for all requirements.

Comfortable seating is the first consideration – this may mean flexible modular units, two or three sofas, some extra chairs, maybe some folding pieces or floor cushions. The amount of furniture depends on the size and shape of the room, but avoid creating a cluttered environment. Encourage members of the family to try out seating to make sure it meets their needs. From a practical point of view think about the safety aspects, particularly in terms of fire, and ease of cleaning. You may also need to include small tables for lamps and other items.

Storage will depend on how you are going to use the room, but the sitting room will probably need to incorporate CDs, cassettes and video and television, so you will need to include these in your plans when looking at your use of space. Any large pieces of furniture should be sited some distance from the seating and the fireplace.

The furnishings in the sitting room may reflect the style of the room, but considerations such as comfort should also be prime.

Health point
Avoid unsafe upholstery and materials such as inflammable foam fillings in sofas and chairs. Put a fireguard in front of an open fire.

Back problems are only too common so good seating should be a priority. Choose chairs according to need – firm-backed chairs that support your back when eating or working, a comfortable but supportive armchair with arm rests for relaxing.

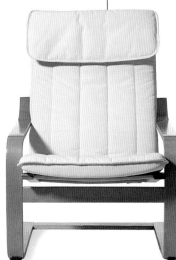

FENG SHUI SITTING ROOM

South-west facing rooms are favoured here because this direction is said to encourage good relationships, but within the room your aim should be to create a spacious, comfortable and relaxed atmosphere. Rounded-shaped seating promotes relaxation, and enables a smooth circulation of energy. For relaxation too, it is important to avoid clutter.

Create a balanced seating arrangement, possibly grouped around a table, with separate pieces slightly angled rather than positioned directly opposite each other, which can be confrontational. The shape and size of your seating can vary, provided the overall effect is balanced. In a particularly large room, you may be able to separate the room into different areas, perhaps one for conversation or family discussions with chairs in a companionable circle, and another area for television or games.

Avoid creating sharp angles in the room with a corner cabinet while providing extra storage space

Use warm welcoming colours to create a friendly atmosphere

Healthy plants and flowers encourage energy to flow

Choose curtains that harmonize with other furnishings in the room

Chairs placed in a circular arrangement create a more harmonious atmosphere

Energy can flow freely into an uncluttered area of the room

Round tables allow energy to flow uninterrupted

How you place your furniture in your sitting room can drastically affect your feng shui. Just making a simple rearrangement of the chairs in the seating area and adding a round table rather than a rectangular version can create more satisfactory energy flows.

Coping with the television

Television can be a favoured source of family entertainment and information; it can also, and frequently does, create problems, disrupting conversations and causing tensions. Its presence too can have an almost hypnotic effect. For these reasons, it is advisable to make the television as unobtrusive as possible, perhaps even placing it in closed, or open-shelved storage when it is not being used.

A confrontational seating arrangement with occupants directly facing one another

An angular occasional table prevents energy from circulating

A door opening onto the back of the sofa is both irksome and blocks energy flows

LIVING SPACES
THE KITCHEN

FOR MOST PEOPLE the kitchen is the heart of the home, and one of the most important rooms in the house. It is here that food is cooked, for entertainment and family meals; it may also be the place where the family gathers, where children do their homework and a variety of tasks are carried out. For others, the kitchen may be less active and more stream-lined, but it still remains fundamental to the home.

You need to analyse your kitchen carefully before you plan how to organize it, bearing in mind how you are going to use it. What-ever solutions you choose, a kitchen must be safe, and there should be separate areas for dif-ferent tasks such as preparing food, cooking, washing dishes, eating, laundry, and so on, so that the individual functions do not conflict with each other.

All kitchens usually need a cooker, sink, fridge and/or freezer and other food storage facilities, work surfaces, and space to use and store kitchen equipment and uten-sils. You may also need to put a dishwasher into the kitchen and a washing machine and dryer, if your home does not stretch to a sepa-rate utility room, as well as a table and chairs, or a breakfast bar and stools for snacks and quick meals.

In order to prepare, cook and store food as well as possible you need to be able to move and work efficiently and safely between the different areas where you are going to carry out the individual tasks. Many people recommend a so-called 'work triangle' so that you

can move easily between the food store, work surface, and cooker. Different forms of this arrangement can be used in a variety of kitchen shapes and sizes, and can incorpo-rate a sink or dishwasher.

Within a healthy kitchen too, all surfaces, particularly stove top, sink, draining boards and work sur-faces, must be kept clean. Ceramic tiles, marble, enamel and stainless steel surfaces can all help hygiene.

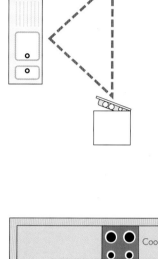

The 'work triangle' shows placement of kitchen appliances for maximum efficiency and preparation space.

With easy-to-clean work surfaces, good storage and sharp knives out of reach, this kitchen/breakfast room is safe and functional.

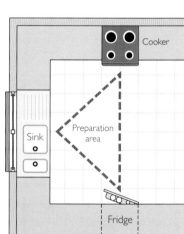

FENG SHUI

In feng shui, the kitchen is not only the place where food is stored and prepared, it is also associated with healing, well-being, and may also reflect or influence the wealth or status of the family. It should be kept clean, uncluttered, and the positioning of objects should encourage a good energy flow; rounded edges for kitchen surfaces are recommended, rather than sharp edges or angles, which can cause disharmony.

Positioning kitchen equipment, particularly the stove, reflects the principles of the Five Elements. For harmony, therefore, the stove or cooker, as a fire element, should be placed some distance from the fridge and sink, both of which are water elements. In a feng shui kitchen, the cooker or hob is the most important appliance of all. It can be placed in the centre of the kitchen, so that the cook looks out into all areas of the kitchen and is never startled while cooking. If, for any reason, you need to place your cooker against a wall, and your back therefore faces the door while you are cooking, you should hang a mirror above the cooker which will then enable you to look into the room as you work.

Health point

Keep work surfaces and utensils spotlessly clean. Store sharp and heavy objects, such as knives, scissors and pots, in cupboards. Avoid slippery floor surfaces. Keep children away from stoves and point pan handles away from stove edges. Check food regularly to make sure it is fresh.

All sharp objects should be kept hidden; knives could be kept in a block or drawer

The best place to position the sink is under a window. This sink is also sited away from the cooker, avoiding a clash of fire and water elements

An extractor hood will help to remove excess heat and damp from the kitchen and avoid it spreading to other areas of the house

Good energy flows are maintained if surfaces are uncluttered

Ideally a mirror should be placed above this cooker so that the cook can see anyone coming into the kitchen through the door behind

Use shelves to display your favourite, attractive china to add welcoming colour to the room

Cork is an ideal flooring – it is warm both to walk on and in colour and is easy to clean

Cupboards should be used to store all kitchen equipment, avoiding clutter, and should be kept closed

Following a few simple feng shui rules when designing the kitchen can influence the health, wealth and harmony of family members.

CLEANSING SPACES
BATHROOMS AND LAVATORIES

BATHROOMS SHOULD be pleasant places, where you can start the day in a positive mood, and end the day in a relaxed frame of mind. The way you plan space here must reflect individual needs – whether the family contains small children, or elderly people, for instance – and the size and amount of any fitted equipment such as bath, basin and bidet.

Your house may have just one bathroom, which contains a lavatory, or there may be two separate areas. You may even have more than one bathroom, in which case each room may have slightly different purposes. A guest bedroom, for instance, may have an ensuite bathroom, which is rarely used.

No matter how many bathrooms you may have in the house, you will need clever planning in order to fit in all the necessary items, and to maintain a tidy and uncluttered environment. This is one area where paper planning and careful measuring can be very

useful. It can be particularly helpful to plot the plumbing positions on your original plan, to ensure that new basins, baths and so on are sited as efficiently and comfortably as possible.

In a fairly large bathroom you may have room to incorporate a separate shower or you may even be able to site it elsewhere in the house. If this is not possible, you may choose to install one over the bath. Showers are refreshing and efficient, but it is as well to resist the temptation to replace a bath with a shower, because there are times when you will want to relax and have a long soak.

Bathrooms lend themselves to clutter, which should always be avoided. Think about using wall-mounted cupboards as 'closed' storage, above the lavatory, bidet or basin – above head height of course – or shelves for display purposes. You may also be able to use space under the bath, adding special side panels if you want to keep the items dust-free.

Windows are an important feature for fresh air as well as natural light. Sheer curtains (below) or opaque glass (above) will let in light while maintaining privacy.

Placing plants in the bathroom helps create a lush, relaxing atmosphere. The fern family offers a variety of plants which thrive in high humidity and shade.

FENG SHUI By definition, bathrooms and lavatories are associated with the water element, and are considered to be difficult rooms in feng shui. Water is obviously cleansing, and the two rooms are primarily concerned with removing waste, but water, and elimination, can also flush or drain away energy, wellbeing, and possibly even wealth. The correct positioning of the bathroom can do much to counteract this process. Feng shui practitioners would advise against placing a bathroom or lavatory in the centre of the house, next to the kitchen or opposite the front door, because all situations cause energy problems. Most appropriate is a bathroom/ lavatory against one outside wall, preferably in the rear of the house. Alternatively, good ventilation, sunshine, and the use of mirrors to reflect energy back into the room can counteract draining processes.

Where a bathroom and lavatory are combined in one room, it is advisable to plan some device for separating the two spaces. Feng shui practitioners also suggest keeping the lavatory lid down to prevent the loss of wealth. The whole area should be kept clean and fresh, with wooden flooring and plants. Most feng shui practitioners advise against ensuite bathrooms in the bedroom in the belief that they drain the energy from the bedroom.

Health point

Keep medicines and any potentially hazardous objects such as razors and nail clippers in lockable cupboards. Use non-slip mats in the shower and safety glass in a shower door.

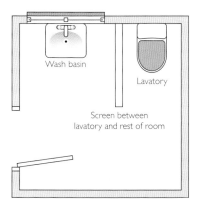

Wash basin

Lavatory

Screen between lavatory and rest of room

For good feng shui, screen the lavatory from the washing area.

White touches offset the power of the black water element.

RESTING
SPACES
THE
BEDROOM

Choose a bed for comfort, size and style, so that it predominates but does not overwhelm the room.

Bedrooms can contain allergens: feathers and down may irritate some people and synthetic fabrics and duvets can also cause allergic reactions. Organic cotton is considered the hypo-allergenic alternative.

A bedside table should be positioned to ensure that light from the lamp falls at a comfortable reading height.

YOUR BEDROOM is one of the most important rooms in the house. You are likely to spend about a third of your life in your bedroom, much of it asleep, and how you sleep and dream will deeply affect your health and life. The bedroom is also where you may be most private, and sometimes most intimate. It is where you dress, undress, store your most personal possessions, and the one place where you should be able to get away from the rest of the house and relax.

These needs should influence the way you organize your bedroom. Your first priority should be your bed – this should be comfortable but firm enough to promote healthy sleep, large and strong enough to accommodate you comfortably, and your partner if you have one. You might choose a simple design, or make your bed a specific feature, but, if so, make sure it does not overwhelm the room.

For relaxation, you could also include a comfortable chair, or a sofa or chaise-longue in a large room. You could place this parallel to the foot of a double bed. You may also need a small occasional table to hold a lamp, making sure that the height is correct to allow you to read comfortably in bed. Book shelves, possibly a desk, bedside tables or lockers can all be useful, as can an attractive chest of drawers.

Some people also like to introduce a wash basin or ensuite shower into the bedroom, which can ease pressure on the family bathroom, but be careful not to impose too much on the space.

Your aim should be to create a tranquil environment so that you wake up refreshed rather than tense. Be careful about how you store possessions. As the years pass, your possessions – clothes certainly – will increase, so bear this in mind when planning storage. You can create extra storage by placing wardrobes either side of a unit, chest of drawers or dressing table, and linking them with storage cupboards, that could be screwed to the ceiling. Avoid doing this over the bedhead, however, as it can cause headaches and a feeling of being boxed in.

Space is often available under beds where pull-out drawers can be the practical answer. In small rooms, particularly children's rooms, you could use a split-level solution, raising the bed above cupboards, a desk or hanging space.

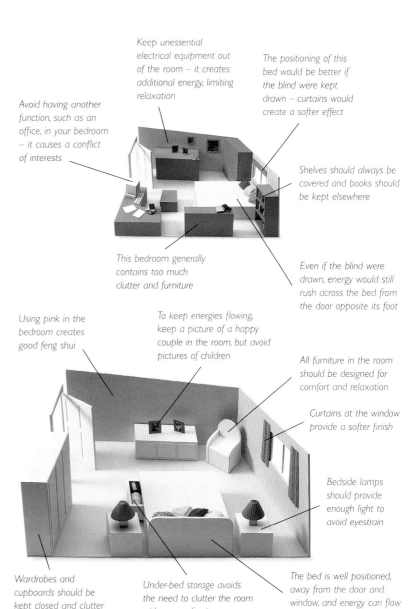

Keep unessential electrical equipment out of the room – it creates additional energy, limiting relaxation

The positioning of this bed would be better if the blind were kept drawn – curtains would create a softer effect

Avoid having another function, such as an office, in your bedroom – it causes a conflict of interests

Shelves should always be covered and books should be kept elsewhere

This bedroom generally contains too much clutter and furniture

Even if the blind were drawn, energy would still rush across the bed from the door opposite its foot

Using pink in the bedroom creates good feng shui

To keep energies flowing, keep a picture of a happy couple in the room, but avoid pictures of children

All furniture in the room should be designed for comfort and relaxation

Curtains at the window provide a softer finish

Bedside lamps should provide enough light to avoid eyestrain

Wardrobes and cupboards should be kept closed and clutter hidden

Under-bed storage avoids the need to clutter the room with excess furniture

The bed is well positioned, away from the door and window, and energy can flow freely

FENG SHUI BEDROOMS

Here too the bedroom is the most intimate room in the home. It needs to be calm, relaxed and safe. Clutter must be avoided. Feng shui practitioners would strongly advise against using the bedroom as an office, or even, in some cases, keeping books in the bedroom, because they can introduce a working element and therefore confusion.

Furnish to provide as uncluttered an effect as possible and avoid sharp-cornered furniture near the bed, as it can break up energy flows. Consider instead rounded edges for built-in furniture and circular bedside tables. The bed must be comfortable, ideally made of wood with linen sheets, and a natural-fibre mattress. Choosing the right bed can revitalize your energy, revive a relationship and bring a couple back together.

Ideally position your bed diagonally opposite the bedroom door, with the headboard against the wall. Like this you will be well grounded and free from draughts, but energy can flow freely around the room. Goods such as bedding, towels and blankets can be stored in drawers under the bed but avoid enclosing your head space with storage; this will disrupt sleep and cause headaches.

RESTING SPACES
CHILDREN'S BEDROOMS

A child's bedroom has to grow and develop with the child. It may begin as a nursery, used for sleeping, changing, bathing and feeding, and evolve through various stages into an almost self-contained teenage space. Furniture needs to be flexible and long-lasting and storage planned with the future in mind. Decorate major surfaces so that they are practical, hard-wearing and easy to redecorate. Colours will change at each stage of the child's development. Use attractive strong pastels for the nursery stage, bold primary colours for toddlers and more relaxing schemes when the school and homework stage is reached. Teenagers are bound to have their own ideas about decoration. Floor coverings should be practical but warm and comfortable underfoot. Paint is the most practical wall-covering; woodwork and furniture can also be decorated in order to create a contrast.

Use these stage-by-stage guidelines for a bedroom that will 'grow' with the child.

The nursery: plan for a crib, nursing chair, changing surface, large cupboard with hanging space, and shelves for small garments.

Toddler's room: remove the crib and nursing chair; add a cot, large toy box, blackboard or other drawing surface. Put a pinboard above the play and painting surface, formerly the changing table. Add bookcase or shelves.

Schoolchild's room: remove cot, alter hanging space, place more shelves in the wardrobe, convert the play top to a desk, and create a split level with some storage under a bunk bed.

Study-cum-bedroom: split the bunks into single beds, place a bedside table between them; add shelves above the desk, and add a pair of director-style chairs or cushions for visiting friends.

Teenage room: replace bunks and storage drawers with a single or sofa bed; convert wardrobe to all-hanging space; add a new chest of drawers; make dual-purpose desk/dressing table with free-standing or wall-mounted mirror.

Young children's bedrooms should be light, cheerful and free of any toxic materials such as lead-based paint. All furniture, furnishings and toys should conform to recognized safety standards.

FENG SHUI CHILDREN'S BEDROOM

Here the emphasis is on creating a place where a child or young person can escape from the ever increasing demands of the outside world. A child's bedroom should be a place for relaxation and inspiration. For this reason, feng shui does not recommend too many primary colours; instead the emphasis is on harmonizing colours, natural fabric toys, and a feeling of softness, light and space. The room should contain positive and inspiring pictures, perhaps of the natural world; well-placed mobiles to keep energy moving; soft lighting and airy window coverings. Feng shui also recommends wicker baskets or a traditional toy chest in preference to plastic stacking boxes. Synthetic floorings and fluorescent lighting should always be avoided. Colours will, of course, depend on the preferences of the child, but a yellow shade is usually suitable.

Children accumulate a lot of possessions. As a toddler's room is transformed into a schoolchild's room, bunk beds can save space and provide storage.

Feng shui recommends harmonizing and soothing colours for young people's surroundings. Green plants encourage health, and all furniture and furnishings should be made from natural materials.

CREATIVE
SPACES
THE
WORKROOM

Working from home is stressful when space is limited. A compact work station that contains all needs but takes up little space can be a solution.

HAVING A PERMANENT work space at home is a fairly recent development. Traditionally, large houses had a library, which was usually a male preserve; more modest homes might have had a study. But the current trend towards freelancing and working at home, and the need for children to have somewhere to study away from the centre of family activity, has made a private working space a more common element in many households.

Basic items of equipment might include a desk, ergonomically designed chair, storage equipment, such as shelves or filing cabinets, telephone, fax machine, computer, reference material and desk lamps.

Planning the working space will depend very much on your needs, the type of work you do, and how much space is actually available. It will also depend on what arrangement best encourages a good work flow, and boosts your energy. However, good light, well-designed chairs, unrestricted access to your equipment and reference material, plus the availability of power points and telephone line, obviously all play a part in the organization of the space.

Feng shui practitioners would also recommend a healthy green plant to absorb any pollution, a wooden desk with curved edges, and fresh red flowers to promote clarity of thoughts. Ideally, the desk should

be placed so that your back is against the wall, providing support, and you can see whoever might come in through the door. Any workroom should be kept as clutter-free and organized as possible to prevent tension or irritation, and to encourage clear thought.

In many cases, this sort of working space has to be dual-purpose – not every home can relinquish an entire room – and sometimes a work room has to double as a spare bedroom. When this happens, it is advisable to let the most important use determine how the room is organized; also, if possible, arrange the room in such a way that two separate 'zones' appear to be created.

Using ergonomically designed work stations will help to prevent back and arm ache.

Health point

There is increasing concern, and argument, about the impact of computers on health. Repetitive strain injury (RSI), for instance, which can cause swelling, tenderness and muscular spasms to any part of the upper arm from the elbow to the fingers, is said to be caused by keyboarding. To counteract possible ill-effects make sure you use good seating, specially designed keyboards, and the correct height of work surface. You should also take frequent breaks away from the computer screen.

**Plants provide a
healthy
environment in
which to relax.**

CONSERVATORIES

ADDING AN EXTRA SPACE to a house in the form of a conservatory is a relatively recent development. But it is a very exciting one. Creating a conservatory or sun room can give a sense of extending your house into the outdoor environment, giving you an area of sun and light, where you can grow plants and sit and enjoy a restful environment.

But, before taking such a step, you do need to work out exactly how you want to use a conservatory – as a greenhouse, summer dining extension, or even a type of play or games room. It is usually advisable to use professionals for extension work but do think carefully before calling in experts and obtain more than one financial estimate before making any decision. Alternatively, you can obtain pre-fabricated conservatories and do the building work yourself, but bear in mind the need for any foundation.

When planning a conservatory, remember too that it can cut the light from the room or corridor from which it leads, even though it is a glazed building; take this into consideration when you are siting the conservatory, and when you are choosing colours. The access to the extension will automatically become the way through to the garden, so choose flooring with care – it needs to be hardwearing and washable and should ideally be a natural flooring of stone, slate, terracotta or quarry tiles, which can then be softened with some form of matting.

Think about safety too. Use double-glazed panes, which can have insulated blinds sandwiched between the layers, and a double layer of transparent roofing material. Some conservatory roofs are made of glass, in which case this should be a special safety or wired glass; some are made of transparent plastic, and again thought should be given to safety, in case of a heavy snowfall, or debris falling onto the roof in bad weather. Laminated glass is recommended for vulnerable areas such as the entrance door.

Building a conservatory obviously changes the shape and dimensions of your home, and this must be considered before taking what is a fairly major step. Feng shui practitioners strongly advise that you consult a feng shui master before possibly unsettling home and fortune with an extra dimension.

If your home is becoming cramped, and you have the space and budget, a conservatory or sun room can provide an extra area that is ideal for relaxation.

Take into account the many ways you may want to use your conservatory – as a greenhouse, study or games room – in order to design the perfect space.

Depending on your taste and budget, you can opt for the cool elegance of a large Raj-style conservatory or a more simple sunny, plant-filled extension. Both create health-giving links with nature.

LIGHT

Light and life go hand-in-hand. Nothing is more conducive to a healthy home than good light or lighting. In Scandinavia, for instance, the arrival of snow is greeted with pleasure because the light available increases as it is reflected off the snow. We need clear natural light from the sun to raise our spirits and make us feel good; in fact, research increasingly shows how lack of daylight can cause emotional and other problems such as depression or seasonal affective disorder (SAD). Light can do much to counter these problems. As it changes during the day natural light can affect mood from energetic enthusiasm in the morning, to a calmer, more reflective mood in the evening as the sun goes down. The presence of natural light in the home also provides a pleasing link between indoors and outdoors.

So, when you are planning your home, you should think about allocating rooms according to the amount of natural light they receive, as well as for other practical reasons. The traditional artists' studio, for example, usually had a large north-facing window, so that the painter had as pure and cool a light as possible to avoid distorting colours on the canvas. Morning light is brighter and clearer than afternoon or evening light, which has a more mellow, yellowish cast, so east-facing rooms are cheerful ones to wake up in, or to eat breakfast. By contrast, a warm evening light will be comfortable and relaxing for a night-time sitting room.

Obviously, however, as the day wears on, natural light fades and we need to use artificial lighting. There is an enormous range of artificial lighting available today and you need to plan your lighting just as carefully as any other structure or service in your home so that it is an integral part of your environment. Thinking about the direction, strength, and type of lighting that you are going to use, and where you are going to site cables, light fittings and sockets, is just as important as any other decorative feature. The way you use different lighting is an essential part of creating a healthy home environment; if planned wisely, daylight and artificial light can complement each other.

Lighting, like colour, creates both mood and atmosphere, and needs to be thought about carefully. It has the ability to dazzle or enhance, dim or brighten any space. Light and colour are closely integrated; the amount of light a colour receives can change its appearance subtly, so the two should always be considered together.

INTRODUCING MORE LIGHT

Sunlight streaming through a well-placed stained glass window helps to brighten a dark stairway and throws interesting shadows onto the floor.

Blinds diffuse direct sunlight, which can cause uncomfortable glare, to create a more muted, softer light. Shiny surfaces, such as glass and chrome, reflect light and add brightness but can be dazzling.

THERE IS NO SUBSTITUTE for natural daylight; its very presence encourages health and wellbeing. Unfortunately, during winter and in northern climates sunlight can be limited. Low-ceilinged houses with small windows, deep basements, city housing overshadowed by neighbouring properties, and suburban or country houses surrounded by trees may also lack sufficient natural light.

However, there are many ways of encouraging more natural light into the house. Not only will these methods brighten the home but also letting in more light creates a greater feeling of space and reduces reliance on artificial lighting.

Some light-increasing ideas involve structural alterations and building work; others are simpler, more 'cosmetic' changes. Keeping rooms streamlined and free of clutter, for instance, encourages a sense of light. Pale colours and shiny textures reflect light, so using a silky-textured wallpaper or vinyl silk emulsion on walls and/or ceilings will help to brighten a room and create an impression of greater space. So too will gloss paint on woodwork; glazed chintz or silk and satin for curtains; metals such as brass, chrome, silver for curtain poles, furniture frames or accessories. Remember however that too many shiny textures in one room can be disturbing and too dazzling.

Basement apartments are often dark, particularly if overlooked by an exterior wall, which prevents light from penetrating the interior. Painting the outside wall, or the area opposite the window, in white, pale yellow or blue can help to reflect more light through the window. Using these colours too in individual rooms can also help to create a sense of light.

LIGHT THROUGH GLASS

Glass is another light producer. Glass-topped tables on metal legs will look as if they are floating, and help to increase a feeling of spaciousness. Glass shelves placed across a recess, or even across a 'blind' window, lit from above or below, and perhaps used to display a collection of coloured glass or plants will effectively increase light and reflect any sunlight that does come in through the windows.

Stained glass windows or doors also create interesting coloured shadows on walls, ceilings and floors as light shines through them, creating a jewel-like brilliance. Such treatments need to be used with care because too much stained glass or heavy window treatments such as diamond-paned or leaded light glazing can cut natural light and should only be used if they suit the architectural style.

ADAPTING WINDOWS

If you are considering structural changes to your home, you can increase light by replacing existing windows with larger ones, installing energy-saving sealed double- or triple-glazing at the same time. Picture windows and sliding patio doors are particularly effective ways of bringing daylight into the home, but bear in mind the need for environmental harmony, and the architectural style of your property; such additions can bring a jarring note if they are out of style. You can also create spacious and light areas by knocking down interior walls, enabling light to flood into the

Curtains should be
pulled well back to
allow as much light
as possible to enter
a room.

home. This sort of dramatic change, however, needs to be planned with considerable care.

If structural changes are too drastic, then there is much you can do with your existing windows. Obviously well-kept clean windows encourage light in their own right. But you can also let in more light by using curtains or other window treatments creatively. If using lined curtains, place the curtain track or pole fairly high above the window and take it well beyond the curtain frame so that the curtains can be pulled back clear of the window during the daytime. You can also tie them back or fix them out of the way with wall attachments. Pelmets or valances at the top of windows can cut light, so make sure they too are positioned high up, with the lower edge in line with the top of the window frame. Simple blinds such as slatted Venetian blinds or roller blinds are

Adding new
windows encourages
natural light into
the home. A well-
placed window
brightens a
bathroom, skylights
let light into
windowless areas
such as attics or
landings, and French
windows provide a
pleasing link with
the outdoors.

less light restricting and allow you to control and diffuse daylight into the room.

Fine, sheer drapes running from floor to ceiling or wall to wall, in voile, muslin or lace, also diffuse light in interesting ways.

Other ways of increasing a sense of light include using glass bricks as exterior panels in brick walls, or setting glass fish tanks or terrariums into interior walls. These add light, interest, and a feeling of calm. To admit an effective amount of daylight, consider installing lantern lights into the roof, often possible on landings where the extra light will brighten hallways, or by adding sloping roof lights or skylights. You can also provide additional sunspaces by creating a conservatory or an atrium, but bear in mind that an extension can actually cut light or introduce a sense of gloom into the adjoining room.

Light-encouraging tricks

Mirrors are an effective way of increasing light because any reflected light makes a room look larger; glazed pictures and prints can also help. Think carefully about where to position mirrors, perhaps using a helpful partner to judge the effect before committing yourself. You can also do a 'dummy run' with silver foil before hanging the mirror. Remember that a mirror is heavy and so needs to be fixed firmly with special mirror plates and screws, or screwed to the wall with counter-sunk screws, hidden behind domed metal heads.

Mirrors are also an effective way of magnifying artificial light. You can hang mirrors in recesses, lit from above with concealed lighting; placed behind a candle flame or oil lamp, which themselves can be put on a sheet of mirror glass; hung in a hall to enhance the effect of a central pendant light or chandelier, or hung above an attractive fireplace. Mirror tiles, stuck to a wall, also reflect light, but make sure your wall is perfectly smooth, otherwise reflections will be distorted. These tiles can look utilitarian, and are probably best confined to kitchens or hi-tech settings.

Well-positioned mirrors reflect light and bring a feeling of greater space to any room. For best effect, mirrors should be kept clean and sparkling.

NATURAL LIGHT or sunlight is energy in its truest form so that light plays an important part in feng shui philosophy. Feng shui recognizes the need for artificial lighting in certain instances but places greater emphasis on encouraging natural light into the home, or using your home in a thoughtful and creative way to make maximum use of natural light during daylight hours, reserving other sources of light, symbolic of the fire element, to enhance, activate or boost energy levels and lighting when necessary.

In feng shui, sunlight is associated with yang; shade with yin. The aim of feng shui is always to achieve balance and harmony, so when organizing rooms your aim should be to achieve a balance between the amount of sunlight let into a room and the amount of shade that the room receives. Living areas need healthy and bright amounts of sunlight; well-lit living areas encourage good chi or energy flow. However, too much direct sun can cause headaches and oppressive feelings, which can be counteracted by reducing glare and introducing shade, or by hanging a crystal in the window to break up the sunbeams.

The positioning of your home affects the amount of natural light available, and therefore the way energy flows through the home. South-facing rooms receive full light, ideal if you need more fire energy or to activate energy levels. East-facing rooms will receive light from the rising sun; west-facing rooms, light from the setting sun. North- or north-east-facing rooms will not receive much direct light.

Lighting can be chosen according to the element associated with a particular direction; candles could be used in the south

Sunlight is an important factor in the attractiveness of a room, but too much direct sun can fade furniture and cause headaches. Blinds, shades and sheer curtains can diffuse light and create a balance of light and shade.

It is possible to encourage more daylight into your home by some structural changes, but in feng shui such changes will disrupt the balance of the home and need to be considered carefully, perhaps with advice from a feng shui consultant. An alternative is to use different rooms according to the way light changes during the day.

LIGHT ENHANCERS
Feng shui has many ways of encouraging light into the home. The use of beautiful colours, light-reflecting textures and clear space in themselves encourage a sense of lightness. Light-reflecting objects such as crystals or mirrors can be strategically placed to encourage light, boost energy levels and direct energy around the house. By day,

mirrors will reflect natural light; at night, they can maximize light from candles or lamps. Too many mirrors, however, will speed up energy flow, creating hyperactivity and conflict, so they should be used carefully, and should not face each other.

You can also make maximum use of kinetic, or moving, lighting, by installing an open fireplace, using lit candles, especially in the north-east part of the home, which should be used for quiet and contemplation. Candles have a gathering influence and also boost fire energy; placed in water they create a perfect balance between the fire (yang) and water (yin) elements. Not all light comes from the sun, and feng shui also advises making use of moonlight to enhance light in the home.

Moonlight streaming into a room casts a tranquil light over the scene and brings good feng shui.

The elements of fire and water are perfectly balanced when candles are placed in water.

63

TYPES OF LIGHTING

IF WE WERE in complete harmony with our surroundings, we would go to bed when the sun disappears. But this is not the case, and we can increase the hours of lightness, brighten dark areas in the home and encourage positive feelings by using artificial lighting. This may be harsher and brasher than daylight, but it can be directed, diffused and reflected in different ways in order to enhance the home, meet specific needs, and create mood.

There are many different types of artificial lighting, which vary according to function, effect and light source. They also vary according to the type of light fitting. These come in two basic types: structural or architectural, and decorative.

Structural fittings are built into the fabric or structure of the room and are usually quite unobtrusive, providing a light source, but not dominant in their own right. Such fittings include downlighters, spot lights, wall washers, uplighters, and indirect lighting in the form of concealed strip lighting.

Decorative lighting, as its name suggests, not only provides a light source but also a decorative element. It includes table and standard lamps, wall lights, pendants and chandeliers, which are usually chosen to enhance a room's style and to blend with its colour scheme. When choosing lights in this category, always check them during daylight, when light shines onto them, and at night, with light shining through them.

Artificial lighting falls into three main categories: general or background (top); display or accent (centre); and task (right).

Don't try and cope with domestic wiring yourself. Most electrical installations should be done by professionals to prevent the risk of shock, heat build up and possible fire risks.

Spotlight   *Downlight*   *Uplight*   *Strip light*

Lighting is often defined according to function. The main categories are:

General or background lighting, also known as ambient lighting, provides the general lighting for a room, often from a central source.

Accent or display lighting, can be used to highlight particular features. Other categories include kinetic or 'moving' light such as flickering candles or firelight to provide mood and atmosphere and specialist lighting such as garden or security lights and novelty lights.

Task lighting, provides a direct or concentrated source for specific needs such as reading or working in the kitchen

	Light switch
	Recessed low-voltage spotlight
	Transformer
	Wall uplighter
	Floor uplighter
	Floor socket
	Wall socket

Making a lighting plan

If you are designing a lighting scheme from scratch, you may find it helps to produce a plan. Use your house or room plan as a base, placing a tracing sheet overlay onto it, and sketching the room outline. Draw on your proposed light fittings so that they relate to, and harmonize with, the arrangement of each room. For instance, you may want to indicate the placing of a pendant light over a dining table, a desk lamp for a work surface, or kitchen lighting. A plan is most useful for task lighting, but you can also use it to experiment with ways of placing background or ambient lighting, thinking in particular about general safety. You can also position display lighting to focus on any attractive features that you want to enhance. Once you have plotted the positions of your lighting, you can draw in the separate circuits, using different colours for each circuit: red for power supply; green for task lighting; and so on. You can then use this plan to brief an electrician.

Pendant   *Wall light*   *Standard lamp*   *Desk lights*

LIGHT
FITTINGS

This pendant lamp eliminates glare by reflecting light back onto the ceiling.

YOUR CHOICE of light fittings will depend on personal taste, room style and colour, how much light you need, where you want to direct it, and what you want the light to do. In practice, most rooms contain a mixture of light fittings. Lampshades and covers, whether glass, metal, fabric, or other materials, affect the quality of light.

For good feng shui, avoid sharp, angular or pointed light shapes and fittings. These cause disharmony and attract hostile energy, because of the 'poison arrows' that they create.

PENDANTS AND CHANDELIERS provide
general or background lighting. Usually suspended centrally from the ceiling, they can generate a dull and unflattering light, leaving room corners in darkness. Lampshades can counteract this. A wide, conical lampshade reflects light back onto the ceiling; an enclosed shade such as a paper lantern will provide softer lighting and hide the bulb. Some pendants are designed for use over dining tables, when they are best combined with a rise-and-fall fitting. Direct glare and strong overhead lighting should be avoided; they are very oppressive.

Glass chandeliers are particularly elegant. Originally they were candle-powered, and provided a magical light, emphasized by the glittering glass. Converted to electricity, they can be harsh, so need low-wattage candle-type bulbs. In feng shui, chandeliers are held to be auspicious and should be placed in the centre of the home, where they symbolize the earth element.

Effective lighting can transform a room. Experiment with styles – the broad illumination of halogen lamps, light-diffusing wall elements, directional ceiling fixtures – to achieve the desired effect.

The combination of a decorative wall light with direct downlighting creates a dramatic effect.

WALL LIGHTS provide a warm, soft background glow and can be decorative. They need to be sited about two-thirds up the height of a wall. This type of light includes uplighters, usually opaque bowl-shaped fittings, which 'bounce' light off the ceiling; for feng shui, they can therefore direct energy upwards and outwards into all the corners of the room. Some uplighters can be used for display lighting, particularly to provide dramatic light from below; a floor-mounted style, for instance, could be placed under a glass-topped table to light plants.

DOWNLIGHTERS are ceiling-mounted, and usually recessed into the ceiling. They project light downwards onto a horizontal surface, and can be used above dining tables. Several can be used together, possibly with their beams crossed to create a warm, overall glow. They will make a ceiling appear darker and lower. They can be used for background, task and display lighting.

WALLWASHERS are another form of downlighter, generally fixed to the ceiling around the perimeter of the room. They effectively 'wash' walls with light, giving an impression of pushing a wall outwards, so creating a sense of space, useful in a narrow room. Wallwashers can also be used as display lighting for wall hangings, paintings, or attractive items of furniture, or for task lighting.

BUILT-IN INDIRECT LIGHTING provides a comfortable background glow and can also be combined with different architectural features such as coving. It can be positioned above wall-mounted cupboards, to throw light onto the ceiling, or within display cabinets.

Spotlights are often used for task lighting, because they are directional. They may be individual 'eyeball' spots, angled to shine in a certain direction, or clip-on. They can also be combined with a special lighting track, usually ceiling mounted but possibly wall- or floor-mounted. Spotlights are particularly effective in small kitchens where there are several surfaces that need clear light. They can also be used as display lighting to illuminate wall hangings, paintings and so on.

TABLE, DESK AND STANDARD LAMPS are most frequently used as task lighting, sited where they are needed to provide a constant, direct and clear stream of light. Glare and dazzle must be avoided.

Table and standard lamps can also be used for general background glow, and as decorative lighting to enhance a colour scheme, or to introduce contrast.

SHADED FLUORESCENTS are an alternative for task lighting requirements, placed over a workbench in a hobbies area, under top cupboards to light a work surface below, or to illuminate shelves.

A glowing fire is a natural source of indirect light and gives a warm ambience to a room.

LIGHT SOURCES

Thomas Edison (1847–1931) the US scientist who invented the electric light bulb in 1879, leading to the development of a wide range of lighting options in the home.

NIGHT-TIME LIGHTING is much more dependent on the development of technology than any other area of interior design, and for centuries not a lot happened. It is only in the last few decades that domestic lighting has become more adventurous, taking inspiration from display and stage lighting so that low-voltage and other modern lighting techniques have become feasible for use in the home.

Originally an orange glow from firelight or rush lights, primitive oil lamps and candles was the only means of extending daylight beyond dusk, with the light source sometimes magnified by metal or a mirror placed behind it. In some grand 18th century rooms, window shutters were backed with mirror glass, reflecting the glittering light from chandeliers, and so creating the impression of light still shining through the windows.

In 1780 the Argand oil lamp was invented, with a capillary-action controllable wick which made it possible to adjust the light level, which transformed domestic lighting. Gas lighting was developed in the 1850s, first for street lighting, and later for home use. Both inventions brought about enormous social change. By the 1880s, electricity was beginning to supersede gas; it needed an incandescent tungsten-filament electric light bulb to supply the light source.

From those early beginnings has developed a wide range of artificial light sources to be used in the home.

The balance of light from a variety of sources and directions – glass doors, high windows or skylights, recessed downlighting, reflected light from the walls – creates an inviting ambience in harmony with feng shui principles.

INCANDESCENT light is used for much domestic lighting. It has a slightly yellowish cast, providing a warm light, and will provide a 'slice' of uniform light, although the amount of light will depend on wattage and fitting.

TUNGSTEN: the original incandescent tungsten-filament light bulb gave off a harsh crude, white light which was not restful to the eye. Tungsten-filament can also supply a reddish light with a fairly long life; the brighter white light bulb was much more short-lived. Compromise was reached with a bulb which gave off a slightly yellow cast, and is still used today in most domestic light fittings. It tends to make reds, pinks, tans, yellows and neutrals look warmer, but to dull down greens and blues. 'Pearlizing' the bulb can soften the light slightly; silvering it will create a clearer light; coloured bulbs can distort light – and colour schemes – but are useful for creating a specific mood.

TUNGSTEN HALOGEN INCANDESCENT lamps have been developed more recently. The filament in the centre of the bulb is surrounded by halogen gas, which gives a brighter, whiter light, and up to 40 per cent more light than the equivalent tungsten-filament incandescent bulb. It also has longer life – up to 2,000 hours. These lamps are mostly used in spotlights, and uplights, and for garden and security lighting, but must be used with care as they produce a great deal of heat; when used indoors they are best combined with a dimmer switch to control the light level.

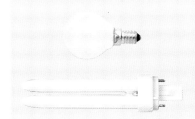

FLUORESCENT lighting provides a flat, cold light which casts few shadows and creates no highlights. Because of its rather cool, unflattering light, various different coloured tubes have now been produced, which give a slightly warmer and pinker light. They are long lasting and energy saving, and some have been adapted into bulb or circular shapes to fit wall lights, table or standard lights, which would normally take only incandescent lights. They tend to give off a harsh light, and an annoying buzzing. They can also cause headaches, eyestrain, and it can therefore be stressful to sit in a room where fluorescent lighting is used. They are probably best used solely for display purposes, but feng shui would advise against their use.

LOW-VOLTAGE lighting is most successful when used to provide accent and display lighting, because it gives a clear and direct light, as well as good colour rendition. The tightly controlled narrow beam can be used to create a dramatic effect; the fittings are discreet and the light is safe and cool to the touch. It is also more economical to run than mains-voltage lighting, although the initial outlay will be more expensive. Low-voltage lighting comes in many forms from downlighters and wallwashers to lamps and uplighters. It is not suitable for general lighting, because of the narrow beam of light that it gives off – but double-focus downlighters, or masses of tiny 'starlights' can be used to provide adequate background lighting.

FULL-SPECTRUM lighting comes in incandescent bulbs and fluorescent tubes, and has been designed to reproduce daylight. Some consider it to be mood-enhancing and beneficial for those who suffer in the absence of sun.

Overcoming SAD
Research shows that moods and behaviour can vary according to season, apparently in response to differing light levels. The most striking effects occur in people who suffer from seasonal affective disorder (SAD), who, every autumn and winter, may experience depression, apathy and tiredness. The mechanisms causing SAD are not yet understood but exposure to bright full-spectrum lamps and specialist daytime lighting can alleviate symptoms.

ASSESSING NEEDS

MOST ROOMS in the healthy home will use several different types of light: general, background lighting; task lighting; accent and display. But how much do you need?

Comfortable light levels are a matter of personal preference. Safety and health are obviously priorities and you will need to light dark corners, changes in floor level and flights of stairs, as well as providing adequate task lighting to avoid eye strain. Fairly bright domestic lighting was once the norm, and is still preferred by many, but the current emphasis is on energy conservation, and the trend is towards clear defined light for working areas, with any surrounding areas more softly lit.

There is also a movement towards greater flexibility in the use of the home. A general-purpose living room for example, needs clear lighting over the dining area while food is being eaten, with the sitting area dimmed to a soft background glow. When the meal is over, the dining area lights can be switched off, or dimmed down, and the lighting in the sitting area can be turned up.

When you are planning how much light is needed for a given activity and area, consider the intricacy of the task to be performed. Close work such as sewing, book-keeping, model-making and so on will require a lot of light. Think too about the colour of the working surfaces; darker materials, and those with little colour contrast, need a higher level of light than black writing on white paper. The eyesight of the person engaged in the task is also important – older people may need more light than those with younger eyes.

Adjusting lighting between one area of a general purpose room and another helps to define areas. Here the dining table (far left) is lit from overhead when in use, while more general lighting levels are switched on when the sitting area is in use (left).

Correct lighting is essential for good health. For close precise work you need clear task lighting to prevent eyestrain.

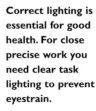

It is also important to avoid glare; too much light coming off a bright, white or shiny surface will tend to contribute to eye strain. It is also essential to light computer and television screens carefully. Reflected light 'bouncing back' will cause distraction. It is often better to place a lamp behind, or to the side of a television set, and to light a computer keyboard but not the screen.

LUX LEVELS AND LUMENS

When measuring light levels, it is usual to consider the light at the point of production, namely the bulb. A candela, the brightness of one candle, is used as the measure of luminous intensity; the lux level, an internationally agreed unit, is used to measure the amount of light falling on any surface. The flow of luminous light from any one source is measured in lumens. The light of one candle has a flow of about 12 lumens; a 100-watt light bulb produces 1,200 lumens.

To measure the light level, add up the number of lumens emitted by all the bulbs in one room. This will give you the overall lumen level, and then you can estimate whether the amount meets your particular needs. The most difficult tasks need about 2,500 lumens; a casual task and general background lighting requires about 1,500 – 2,000 lumens. For close, precise work, therefore, you might need a lamp providing 2,250 lumens above or next to the work area, with a nearby source adding another 750 lumens.

Colour temperature chart measured in degrees Kelvin.

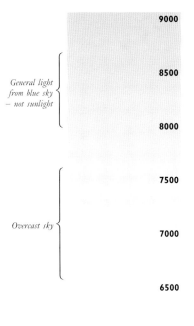

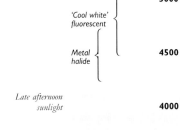
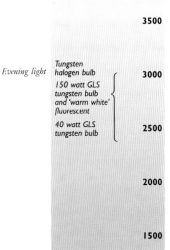

9000

General light from blue sky – not sunlight
8500

8000

Overcast sky
7500

7000

6500

6000

Direct summer sunlight overhead at midday
5500

'Cool white' fluorescent
5000

Metal halide
4500

Late afternoon sunlight
4000

3500

Evening light
Tungsten halogen bulb
3000
150 watt GLS tungsten bulb and 'warm white' fluorescent
40 watt GLS tungsten bulb
2500

2000

1500

The coolness or warmth of light is something else to consider when you are planning your lighting. Natural daylight is the usual point of reference, but some daylight can appear very cool. The light from a blue or overcast sky, for instance, or from a northerly direction is usually much cooler or bluer than the clearer, purer white sunlight overhead at midday.

You can use a Kelvin chart to measure the degree of warmth or coolness in any form of light, both natural and artificial. The scale is measured in degrees Kelvin, which defines the colour 'temperature' of the light, from blue, through white, yellow, orange and red. Artificial light registers 5,000 degrees – cool white fluorescence, through the warmer fluorescents: low-voltage and metal halide lighting, tungsten halogen, then the incandescent **GLS** bulb. One of the warmest is a flickering candle, or the kinetic light of a glowing radiant fire.

Firelight produces a wonderful flickering light, ideal for relaxation and thinking but not suitable for close work such as reading.

LIGHTING ROOM BY ROOM

Wall sconces give dramatic, diffused light, while overhead lamps clearly illuminate the stairs and entrance for safety.

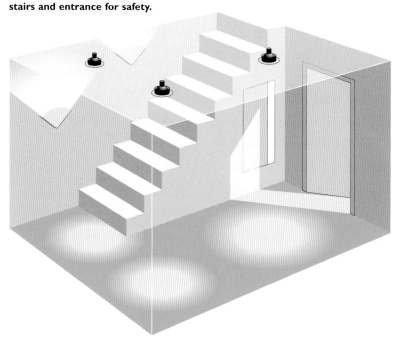

General background lighting with the focus of a pendant lamp over the table gives suitable coverage for a dining room. Remember that a pendant lamp fixed in place can make rearranging the furniture problematic.

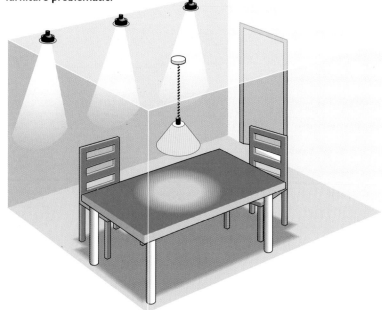

HALLS, STAIRS AND LANDINGS

These areas need to be brightly lit, both for safety and to create a welcoming atmosphere. Stairs must be well lit so that the treads can be seen clearly; a dual switch is advisable linking the hall and landing. The landing light could be on a dimmer switch so that a soft light can be kept on for young children. Table, desks or telephone areas should have separately switched task lighting.

Use wallwashers to focus any architectural features or wall hangings. If the hall is long and narrow, use mirrors to reflect light; hang an eye-catching item on a narrow wall and light it dramatically.

LIVING AREAS

These may be split-function areas. If so the individual areas will need appropriate lighting according to their different function.

Provide soft general background lighting, possibly using a dimmer switch. Use task lighting for reading and games areas, or for any desk area. Light shelves or display cabinets, possibly using integral light. Use accent or display lighting to enhance interesting architectural features.

If one of your rooms doubles as a living space and spare bedroom, make sure that table lamps can be plugged in conveniently as bedside lighting.

DINING ROOM

Provide a soft, background glow, perhaps with integral lighting. Light the dining table clearly, but avoid any glare. You may choose overhead lighting, perhaps a pendant which can be raised or lowered according to what is required. Feng shui warns against using a powerful overhead light as this throws too powerful an energy force onto diners. Candle light on a dining table provides both light and a gathering atmosphere which leads to harmonious socializing.

Food serving areas should be well lit, perhaps with wall lights or lamps which can be switched off or dimmed once the meal is in progress. Use spotlights to focus architectural features, paintings or beautiful objects.

Be sure to provide appropriate task lighting if part of the room is also used as a study.

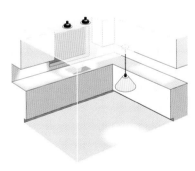

KITCHENS
This is the main 'workroom' of the home. It needs good task lighting, some soft background lighting, and perhaps some accent and display lighting focused on a dresser. Clear, direct lighting is extremely important. Work surfaces and cookers should be well lit from above. Sinks are often placed under a window and receive good natural light during the day; at night, they too will need an extra light source.

Eating areas in the kitchen will need to be well lit, and you can install integral lighting in deep storage cupboards. Power points will need to be seen easily at night.

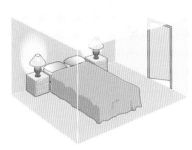

BEDROOMS
The type of lighting will be influenced by the way the room is used. You may need to place nightlighting into a child's bedroom; and task lighting in a room used by a teenager. Bedrooms also need soft, background lighting, best controlled from door and bed. Feng shui experts would strongly advise against siting ceiling lights such as pendant lights directly over the head of the bed, as they will disturb energy.

Bedside lighting can be wall-mounted or an integral part of the bedhead, but should shine onto the pages of a book when sitting up in bed. Feng shui would recommend side lights for reading rather than downlights, which will have a disturbing effect if they pour light onto readers' heads.

Any dressing table area will need good task lighting.

If television is watched in bed, or there is a computer in the room, avoid any light which will cause glare from the screen.

BATHROOMS
Water and electricity do not mix, so safety is of prime importance. Lights should be switched by a pull-cord system, or switches sited outside the bathroom door, fittings should be covered with glass or plastic so that metal parts are unaffected by steam. Many spotlights, uplighters and downlighters are therefore unsuitable for a bathroom. Light any mirror/dressing table area with a clear light which shines onto the face and not the mirror.

Light bath, basin, shower areas well but without dazzle; shiny surfaces can give off glare, and showers in particular need special sealed fittings.

The bathroom is an ideal setting for kinetic lighting in the form of candles or oil lamps. For pure relaxation at the end of the day, you can soak in a bath surrounded by flickering candles.

PLAY AND GAMES ROOMS
These rooms need good background lighting plus some accent or display lighting. Task lighting however will be the most important lighting feature and will depend entirely on how the room is being used.

Desks, play and games surfaces need to be well and separately lit; billiard, table tennis and pool tables need special table lighting.

Safety point

If using candles or oil lamps in the bathroom, make sure they are placed safely and securely and extinguish before leaving.

CONSERVATORIES AND GARDENS

Light fixtures can add hours of use to your conservatory by making it attractive after dark. Choose low-voltage or hydrophonic lighting to assist plant growth, or opt for the natural light of candles.

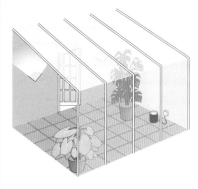

As outdoor lighting gains in popularity, the variety of fixtures increases. Movable lights on spikes and ground-level spotlights can highlight foliage or give added security.

CONSERVATORIES People often forget artificial lighting for conservatories because they receive plenty of natural daylight. After dark, use uplighters for good background lighting, concealed behind or inside plant pots. Also provide adequate lighting for dining and sitting areas. Lighting doesn't need to be electric; the soft glow or flickering flames of candles and oil lamps looks wonderful but do remember to extinguish the flame before you leave. You can use special hydrophonic lighting to encourage plant growth and uplighters or spotlights to feature your plants. Low-voltage lighting is particularly good because it does not become too hot. Make sure that no light is placed too close to foliage where it might cause scorching, or a fire.

GARDEN or outdoor lighting is another increasingly popular type of lighting design. It can be used to emphasize shrubs, trees and other plants, enhance architectural or water features and to create a closer link between your home and your garden. As outdoor entertaining becomes more popular, after-dark lighting also serves a practical purpose.

The golden rule when planning outdoor lighting, however, is that a little light goes a long way; it is essential to plan lighting so that it does not dazzle either yourself or others. Ideally try to plan the lighting at the same time as you plan the garden. At night a 20-watt lamp – even 12 watts—can seem very bright. And a rear garden, however pretty, should be lit with discretion and subtlety if it is not to resemble a football pitch.

As with indoor lighting, fittings and degree of light need to be chosen according to function, whether the aim is security, decoration, task lighting, or simple mood-making.

Your front door and entrance should be well lit, as should any front path, steps, or changes in level. Outdoor or cooking areas also need appropriate lighting; when planning, you may also need to supply garages, summer houses and garden sheds with light and power so that you can use them effectively at night. This may involve running cables from the mains supply, which are usually buried well underground. Any light fixtures you use should also be specifically made for outdoor use, with all metal and electrical parts fitted with anti-glare cowls and louvres to reduce glare.

Some garden lights are low-voltage and can be tucked away discreetly; others are on spikes, which makes them very flexible. You can move them to highlight different plants throughout the year, or to focus on specific areas within the garden.

Candles, lanterns and oil lamps are portable and shed beautiful, natural light indoors or out.

Candles, lanterns and oil lamps are portable and shed beautiful, natural light indoors or out.

Use light to enhance attractive outdoor features such as a gazebo, old wall, garden pool or garden statues. You can also use light to accentuate plants rambling up walls, or trailing down from balconies – white flowers with good green foliage are particularly effective when lit this way, and, as many of these climbing plants such as jasmine or honeysuckle are scented, they will bring an extra pleasure and sensuality.

You can light these features with spotlights, or with downlights, provided you have somewhere to place the fittings such as under the house eaves, in the 'roof' of a gazebo or pergola, or even attached to tree branches. For a softer effect you can use diffused lighting fixed to house or garden walls. Sometimes throwing a tree or other feature into sharp silhouette is even more dramatic and effective; you can achieve this effect by using a spotlight aimed at the fence or wall from close behind the plant.

Strings of lights too, either decorative mini-lights such as those used for outdoor decorating or even strings of coloured 'fairy' lights, can all look magical in the garden if strung between trees, or over a trellis. They also light a dining area subtly if there are enough trees, or the area has its own pergola or awning.

But not all garden lighting has to be electrical. Kinetic lighting can be very effective and creates fascinating plays of light. Candles,

Safety point

Make sure any changes of level in the garden are well lit to avoid accidents. Garden and conservatory light fittings and electric cables must be designed for outdoor use; fittings must be kept moisture free.

oil lamps or storm lanterns can be placed on tables and walls or can even be wall mounted to wonderful effect. Garden flares, usually on long spikes, can be pushed into the earth where appropriate.

Swimming pools and water features should always be carefully lit, because of the potential danger of electricity combined with water. Security lighting is usually controlled with a sensor, which comes on as a person approaches, but some are so sensitive they are set off too easily, causing annoyance and light pollution. An alternative is timed security lighting which can be sited near to the front and back door, or near a garage.

All artificial outdoor lighting should be controlled from inside the house; in some cases however, it is wise to have it dual switched, so you can dim the garden when you are outside if you feel that the light is too bright.

One of the earliest forms of artificial lighting, candles produce a wonderful kinetic light that, in feng shui, is considered to produce a 'gathering' energy, drawing people to the light source.

COLOUR

Life without colour, with everything seen in monochrome, is inconceivable. Imagine a world that did not contain multi-coloured rainbows, dramatic sunsets, or the brilliant colours of plants and insects. Colour affects us emotionally, physically and spiritually. Colour stimulates our senses, encouraging us to relax or be active. Some colours can make us feel hot or cold, happy or sad. Others can even persuade us to eat by inducing an appetite for food.

Colour, wellbeing and emotions are closely linked, and our reactions to colour are often deep and intuitive. It affects not only how a room looks but also how it feels. Think how differently you might feel in either an all-black or an all-yellow bedroom. The colours you choose to decorate your home will reflect you as a person. They will also help you to create a specific mood, ambience or atmosphere in which you can relax, work or entertain. Colours can also play eye-deceiving tricks, making a large room seem smaller and cosier, or a small room calm and more spacious. You can use colour to focus attention on good features and disguise or camouflage less attractive ones.

For these reasons, colour is one of the most important aspects of your home, yet in itself it costs very little. It is no more expensive to create a particular scheme that is stimulating and exciting, or calming and relaxing, than to make random use of colour resulting in a boring or a negative effect that may make you feel uncomfortable, depressed or ill at ease.

DYES AND PIGMENTS

Paint pigments today allow for a greater degree of accuracy in paint mixing than could be achieved with natural sources.

Greek columns

Murex shell

Dyes and pigments came originally from natural sources. Imperial purple, for instance, came from the crushed fragments of the murex whelk; woad produced a blue. Early use of bright colours is now superceded by traces of faded elegance.

Woad

The colours we use for decoration or interior design are usually created by using pigments, dyes and glazes – the basic ingredients that give a surface its colour. Originally these could only be obtained from natural sources – plants, minerals, the earth, animals and insects – which were ground up and suspended in a suitable medium such as oil, animal fat or spirit.

The famous Tyrian purple, the colour used for the Roman Emperor's toga, came from a shellfish, the murex whelk, which, when crushed, gave up a drop of whitish liquid that was used to saturate the cloth; when the liquid dried in sunlight, it turned a deep reddish-purple. Indigo too was the result of a colour change. Made from wood ash, leaves and urine, it appeared pale yellow until exposed to the sun.

Early pigments and dyes were not colour-fast, and faded or greyed over time. Many stately homes or historic buildings looked at today seem to have been decorated in subtle or shabby chic tones, giving quite the wrong impression of the original architect's or designer's intentions. Scottish architect Robert Adam, for example, used strong jades and magentas; Sir John Soane combined rich Indian reds with strong sulphur yellow; and the Ancient Egyptians, Romans and Greeks used bright, bold colour combinations. But when we look at their work today, after centuries of exposure to the elements, we see a pale imitation of the original.

Some past 'recipes' for specific colours contained highly toxic ingredients. For example, a particularly fierce green used in fabric and wallpaper and popular during the late 18th and early 19th centuries contained arsenic; as a result,

many fabric dyers and wallpaper hangers became ill, and some even died because they had been exposed to this fatal substance. Other materials that are used in manufacture, such as lead in paints and asbestos in buildings are also now known to present serious health hazards, so extreme care has to be taken if these are found to be still present in a building today.

As manufacturing processes improved, ready-mixed paints appeared, having previously been mixed by the decorator on site, machine-woven fabrics became widely available and wallpapers were printed by roller, instead of being hand-blocked. The pigments and dyes also improved, but they were still not necessarily colour-fast.

As a result of modern technology, it is now possible to re-create the original colours of the past. Slivers of paint, small scraps of wallpaper and tiny threads of fabric can be put under a microscope and analysed; the resulting 'recipe' enables the colour to be copied accurately, using modern healthier materials.

Modern science has also helped to develop safe sophisticated colouring and dyeing methods. It is estimated that more than three million dyes and pigments have now been created, many of them from petroleum products. Chemists have experimented with paints, stains and glazes and have produced dyes that can be bonded successfully to artificial fibres, enabling an unprecedented range of colours, which have influenced both the fashion scene and interior decorating trends.

Unfortunately, most paints available today, having non-renewable origins, can themselves impact on the environment. To balance this, you can also make use of natural materials in the home, such as brick, stone, wood and textiles, to introduce colour to your home.

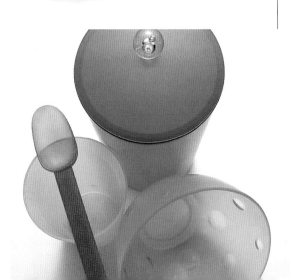

Developments in the chemical industry have produced an enormous range of dyes and colouring processes, resulting in an unprecedented range of coloured paints (far left), fabrics (centre left) and even plastics (left).

THE COLOUR WHEEL

Rainbow

THE COLOUR WHEEL, or colour spectrum, is one of the basic tools that we use to analyse and select colour. Sir Isaac Newton devised the first colour wheel in the 17th century, following his experiments with splitting light, when he discovered the visible spectrum, showing how sunlight breaks down into bands of different wavelengths – the seven colours of the rainbow. Since then there have been other wheels, such as that developed by Johannes Itten of the Bauhaus, but all show the relationship between different colours.

On the wheel, colours are arranged with analogous, or adjacent, colours next to each other, and complementary, or contrasting colours opposite one another. When arranged in the correct sequence, they form a circle.

Pure colours or hues make up the basic wheel. There are 12 of them, and they include primary, secondary, and tertiary colours. They can have white added to them to lighten their value and

create a pastel; grey added to form a mid-tone; or black added to deepen, enrich, and make a shade.

Red, yellow and blue are the primary colours and are equidistant from each other on the wheel. These are the pure, original hues and they cannot be made by mixing together other colours. But when two primary colours are mixed together, they create the secondary colours: blue and red produce violet; blue and yellow produce green; red and yellow produce orange.

When a primary colour is mixed in equal parts with the secondary colour next to it, the tertiary, or intermediate, colours result. These are: blue/violet, red/violet, red/orange, yellow/orange, yellow/green, blue/green and they complete the 12 hues.

The complete colour wheel therefore 'reads': blue, blue/violet, violet, red/violet, red, red/orange, orange, yellow/orange, yellow, yellow/green, green, blue/green – and back to blue.

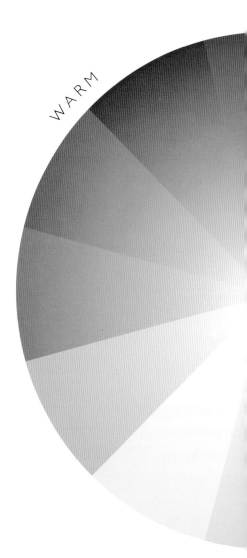

WARM

Colour can change the feel of a room dramatically, so use it according to need. Orange is one of the warm colours and can be vibrant and exciting; green, by contrast, is cool, fresh and elegant.

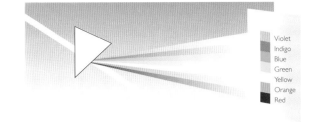

Violet
Indigo
Blue
Green
Yellow
Orange
Red

When white light hits a prism, it divides into the different colours of the spectrum, or rainbow, from red to violet.

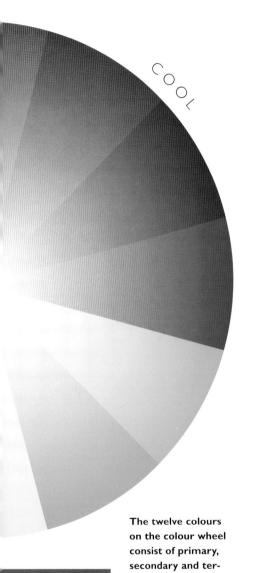

The twelve colours on the colour wheel consist of primary, secondary and tertiary colours. The sequence in which they appear on the wheel clearly shows the natural division between the warm and cool colours.

WARM AND COOL

The wheel divides down the middle with warm or so-called advancing colours on one side. These are the long wave-length colours such as red/violet, red, red/orange, orange, yellow/orange and yellow, which seem to advance or come towards you. Their various tints, tones and shades are also warm – for example, pink, deep rose, and rich burgundy are all values of red and are warm. Apricot, peach and terracotta relate back to orange, whereas gold, lemon and primrose are different values of yellow; they are all on the warm half of the circle.

On the opposite side of the spectrum are the cool or so-called receding colours. These are the short-wavelength colours such as violet, blue/violet, blue, blue/green, green, yellow/green. These colours appear to recede or go away from you. Their various values – lilac, mauve and lavender, for example – are all to be found on the cool half of the colour wheel.

Where the two halves of the wheel join on the 'cusp', on yellow/green and red/violet, colours may be warm or cool, depending on how much of their adjacent colour they contain. For example, some violets are cool when they are mixed with blue, yet are warm when they go towards the red/violet section. Yellow/greens can be warm if there is a lot of yellow in their make-up or cooler when there is more green.

Grading colour

Three characteristics quantify colour: hue, which is the pure colour seen on the colour wheel; chroma or saturation, which is the measure of purity or intensity of the colour; and value (lightness or darkness) of the colour, which is created by adding white, grey, or black to the pure hue found on the spectrum.

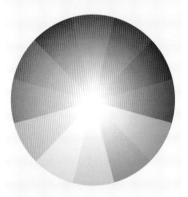

The neutrals

Black, white and grey are, strictly speaking, non-colours, or neutrals. In their pure form, they are added to the different segments of the spectrum to change the tonal value of a colour; that is the way in which a colour is lightened or darkened. Colour tints are created by adding white; tones by adding grey; or shades by adding black. In the home, you can use neutrals singly or together to make a neutral scheme, or individually to create contrast or emphasize a colour scheme

COLOUR PHILOSOPHY

COLOUR PHILOSOPHY is an important feature of feng shui and is closely linked to The Theory of the Five Elements, or energies: Wood, Metal, Fire, Water and Earth. Each of the elements has its own colour. Wood is associated with green, metal with white, fire with red, water with blue or black, and earth with yellow. Each of the colours, like each of the elements, has specific qualities, or fosters certain qualities of life, personality and health. According to Chinese philosophy, each person is born into one of the five elements so that everyone is influenced by one or other of the elements, and the colours they choose, often intuitively, reflect this situation.

Good feng shui strives to achieve balance and harmony and colour plays a major part in this process, aiming to support, boost or move the elemental flow of energy throughout the home.

But unlike conventional interior design, feng shui does not follow specific colour rules. Feng shui practitioners do not automatically recommend that a particular room should be a particular colour. Instead choice of colour reflects a person's birth element and therefore personal needs. A person, for instance, born into the fire element, may need to bring more red into the home to boost their energy needs; while someone born into the wood element, may favour touches of green.

Given the way in which the five elements act on each other, people born into one element may need to take care when using colours associated with another element.

Individual colours too have symbolic significance and feng shui practitioners may suggest using colours to reflect that significance, or enhance possible goals. The colour black, for instance, signifies business success; red promotes luck, growth or happiness; pink can be a healing colour. The significance, however, does not necessarily mean that the colour should be used excessively. Sometimes just a touch – perhaps in the form of flowers, or accessories – may be enough to boost energy or bring that element into the home.

WATER

WOOD

FIRE

METAL

EARTH

The five elements interact creatively or destructively. In this creative cycle each element supports or boosts the next. Colours used in this balanced way will promote health and harmony.

METAL → WOOD → EARTH → WATER → FIRE → (METAL)

Here the cycle is destructive. Colours used like this, for instance by putting too much blue (water) into a red (fire) environment, will create chaos and ill health.

COLOUR
AND
LIGHT

We see colour everywhere in the natural world – the changing hues of the sky from the blue of noon to the reds and purples of sunset, or of vegetation from the fresh greens of spring to the vivid russets of autumn. But colour is simply how our brain perceives different wavelengths of light hitting the eye's retina.

The colour of any surface is influenced by light as well as by the pigments, dyes or glazes which are used to colour it. These are compounds that absorb light of particular colours efficiently and selectively, reflecting it back and determining the specific colour we see. Colours themselves are sensations that result from light of different wavelengths reaching the eye, which sees an object only by the light it reflects. Red is the longest wavelength that we can see; blue and violet the shortest. Some objects reflect and absorb light of different wavelengths equally well: black velvet absorbs nearly all the light which falls on it, reflecting only about 5 per cent back, so it appears dark and dull; white snow

reflects nearly all light that falls on it, so it looks white and shiny.

This can also be explained in the terms of a glowing red sunset. At the end of the day, as twilight falls, the changing colour of the sky is caused by the changing angle between the sun and earth. As the earth turns eastward, and the sun sinks below the horizon, its rays travel further through the atmosphere to reach us. Since there is more atmosphere to travel through, there are more particles to scatter the light. Shorter wavelengths, such as blue, are filtered out, leaving the longer red or orange wavelengths. The same effect can be created at dawn as the sun rises in the east, but it is never as rich a red as in the evening.

The same principles apply in the home. If an item is lit by a pure white light, or seen in daylight, then the colour will be more or less pure. But, if the light source is yellowish, blueish or greenish, it appears to alter the colour. As a result, the same object looks quite different when hit by different light sources. A red cushion, for instance, appears red in daylight or when lit by a red light because it reflects only red light, and absorbs all the other colours. At night, or when lit by a blue light, the same object will

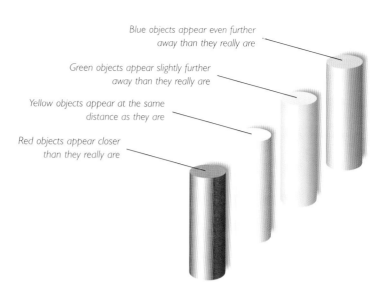

Blue objects appear even further away than they really are

Green objects appear slightly further away than they really are

Yellow objects appear at the same distance as they are

Red objects appear closer than they really are

look much darker, even black. This is why you should always check materials under the exact lighting conditions where they will be used, because they will look quite different in daylight and at night, under artificial lighting.

Short- and long-wavelength colours

Different colours can look slightly closer or further away than they really are – perhaps because of the way each colour is focused on the eye's retina.

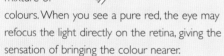

Red light is naturally focused at a point behind the retina when there is a mixture of colours. When you see a pure red, the eye may refocus the light directly on the retina, giving the sensation of bringing the colour nearer.

Yellow light is the colour we see as brightest. It is focused directly on the retina, and so appears neither to advance like red nor recede like blue.

Blue light is naturally focused at a point in front of the retina when there is a mixture of colours. When you see a pure blue, the eye may refocus the light directly on the retina, giving the sensation of pushing the colour further away.

Colour vision depends on the millions of light-sensitive cells that line the retina, the back of the eye, and send signals to the brain whenever they are hit by light rays. There are actually two kinds of cell: rods and cones. The rods only react to light and shade and are sensitive even to very dim light. It is the cones that tell you what colour light is. Cones are less sensitive, which is why your colour vision goes in dim light. There are probably three different kinds of cone, each sensitive to one of the three primary colours. The colour we see depends on how much each kind is stimulated. But there may also be cones that detect the balance between red and green light or yellow and blue light.

It is easy to see the effect of texture on colour by comparing these widely different materials of matching cobalt blue.

Bright daylight shows up the different textures in a room of simple colour palette – predominantly dark blue and white. The interest and variety is created by the juxtaposition of coarse with smooth, glossy with matt, silky with basket-weave. The colour and texture of straw and sponge provide a natural complement.

COLOUR AND TEXTURE

SURFACE TEXTURES can also affect the way we perceive colour – many textures reflect light; some absorb it; others filter and diffuse light. Consequently, the same colour, created by identical 'ingredients' in either the pigment or dye, can appear quite different, depending on the way the surface reacts to the light. You can use this to good effect in the home, incorporating textures into your colour schemes and using them to create mood. It is also another reason why you need to look at fabrics, paint, and other colour samples under the lighting conditions in which they will actually be used.

Many people think of texture purely as a raised, rough or sculpted surface, but these are heavily textured materials. All surfaces have a texture, even if it is perfectly smooth and bland, such as flat, plastered walls that have been painted with matt emulsion paint. This sort of texture tends to absorb light slightly, making the colour look a little weaker or more subtle. The same colour on a shiny, reflective surface, such as gloss paint, silk fabric, or glazed tiles, will look brighter and stronger, as the light is bounced back.

ROUGH TEXTURES

The rough and rustic textures of exposed brick or stone walls, hefty planks of wood, natural floor coverings and coarsely woven textiles absorb light, and so make the colour appear darker, richer, or in some cases duller. Light-diffusing textures, such as sheer muslin and voile fabrics, allow the light to pass through them, making the colour appear softer, more delicate and more subtle.

Heavily textured items can create very interesting effects. Because of their uneven surface, light is reflected, absorbed and deflected differently across them resulting in 'shadow play' from the varying values of the colour. The overall effect suggests a self-coloured but patterned item. You can use this effect in a room where you want to add an extra visual element or dimension but do not want to use a deliberate bold design.

All materials have texture – even if they are perfectly smooth.

Terracotta tiles provide a rich, earthy base for a room.

The pattern of knotty wood gives visual interest while remaining in the background. The uneven visual image contrasts with the wood's smooth texture.

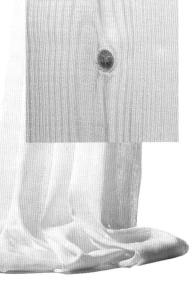

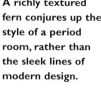

A richly textured fern conjures up the style of a period room, rather than the sleek lines of modern design.

Heavy velvets, brocades and silks give a sumptuous, period feel to a room. Textures, like colours, can be dominant and overpowering or light and soft, creating different atmospheres and moods.

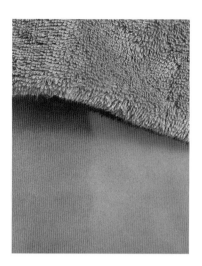

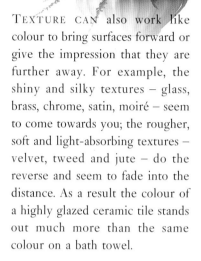

TEXTURE CAN also work like colour to bring surfaces forward or give the impression that they are further away. For example, the shiny and silky textures – glass, brass, chrome, satin, moiré – seem to come towards you; the rougher, soft and light-absorbing textures – velvet, tweed and jute – do the reverse and seem to fade into the distance. As a result the colour of a highly glazed ceramic tile stands out much more than the same colour on a bath towel.

SETTING A STYLE
Texture can also help to set the style of a room – for example some textures are definitely more traditional, and suited to period room settings, than others. Brass, gilt, velvet, brocades, lime-washed walls, weathered beams, sumptuous silks, lace and feathery ferns, for example, all have a period feel, while chrome, especially if combined with smoked glass, brushed aluminium, black ash, hessian, gloss-painted metal, slatted Venetian blinds, all have a more modern image. Some textures, however, such as leather, sheer fabrics, brick and stone, are

When you are working out a colour scheme and you find it lacks texture, or for that matter tonal or colour contrast, you can bring in extra colour by introducing so-called accents. These are accessories, or multicoloured items, such as cushions, wall hangings, pictures, rugs or ornaments, which you can add later to provide contrast.

Plain, natural
materials, such as
cork tiles and
wooden furniture,
offset by a deep red
wall and light-
diffusing blinds create
a harmonious and
healthy living space.

In order to judge different textures
you need to consider the overall
effect the surface will create, and
use as large a sample as possible
when doing your colour-matching.

timeless; it is the way they are used that creates a specific look.

It is very important to achieve textural balance when selecting materials. This means choosing a variety of different textures within the scheme, which will complement and contrast with each other while at the same time relating to the overall style.

SOFTENING TEXTURE

Shiny textures are very 'busy' and stimulating and can almost be disturbing if too many are used in one room. This often happens in bathrooms and kitchens. You can create a calmer feel by balancing shiny textures with soft and delicate light-filtering textures.

The rough, rustic and 'brutal' textures can be very harsh. You need to soften them with some delicate light-filtering surfaces, and bring in emphasis with some sharp metallic effects.

The softer and light-absorbing textures can sometimes appear claustrophobic, especially if they are on a dark-coloured surface. They will look more effective if you contrast them with silk, shiny and light-diffusing textures.

Colour, like sunlight, is a strong mood-enhancer. Wearing favourite colours, or surrounding yourself with them, is a quick and easy way to lift your spirits.

Hospitals and spas use colour therapeutically – light, cool colours have a calming effect, while warm yellow tones can ease arthritis. This soothing environment is enlivened with an arrangement of red flowers.

FROM FENG SHUI through to modern colour therapy, colour has long been associated with healing. The use of colour to heal both physical and emotional ills probably dates back to the very earliest of times, and many ancient cultures believed that colour had curative qualities. The ancient Egyptians, for instance, used yellow beryl stone to cure jaundice and had temple-based healing centres. The ancient Indians and Chinese also practised various colour-based treatments.

Today colour therapy, as a natural healing remedy, is becoming increasingly popular for a wide range of illnesses. Most work is taking place in the field of complementary medicine, and it may be some time before it is widely accepted. Colour healing is, however, beginning to find a place in more conventional medicine, most particularly perhaps in the field of light-based technology.

Colour therapy practitioners in both fields are now claiming some success in using colour to treat disorders such as asthma, eczema, arthritis, and even cancer.

The basic idea behind colour therapy is the belief that colours, as vibrating wavelengths, react with the body and enter it, acting on the body's cells and emotions, causing different effects depending on the frequency of vibration. We can absorb energy from colour through our eyes, skin, breath, food and drink, or through meditation and visualization.

Significantly too, colour therapists argue that different colours have different therapeutic effects, depending on their wavelength or their density. Yellow, for instance, is said to be helpful for arthritis; green is said to play a part in destroying cancerous cells. Colours are also being used therapeutically in hospitals, schools, prisons and care homes.

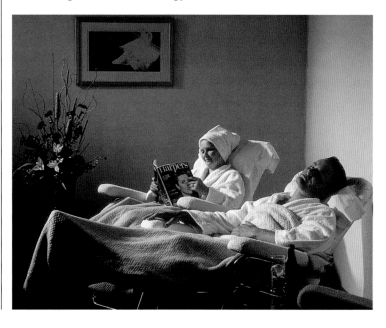

The aura is an energy field. People who see auras describe them as shifting fields of colour pulsing around energy centres of the body.

Outside of medicine, colour counsellors also advise on clothing, food and colours for homes and offices.

According to some colour theorists, colours operate vibrations of high frequency, that can be seen by some people as an aura of glowing colours around a person, or any living thing. Traditionally, the colour of the aura reflects the physical or emotional state of the person it surrounds, and will change colour depending on changes in the person. A healthy, balanced person produces a bright and energetic aura; lack of health produces dullness.

According to different cultures, particularly those of India, the body contains a number of energy points, known as chakras, each of which is associated with a colour. When a person is ill or distressed, the aura becomes imbalanced, and therapy aims to treat the disorder, with the appropriate colour.

Every day of our lives we are surrounded by colour which, if we use it therapeutically, can help us remain healthy throughout our lives.

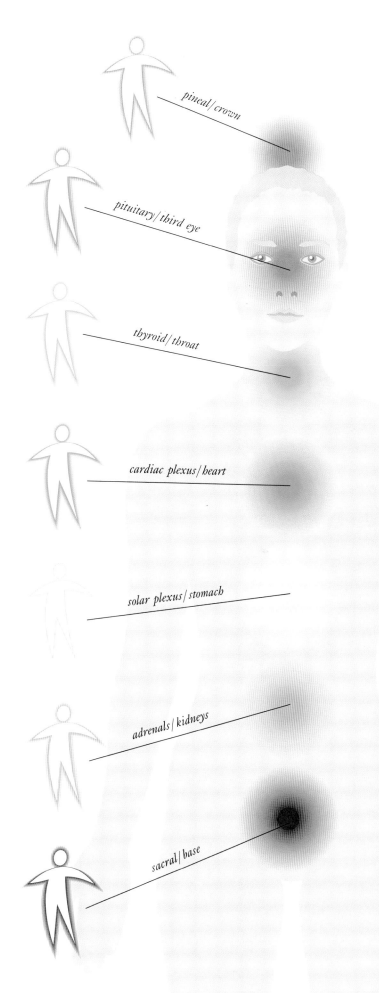

pineal/crown

pituitary/third eye

thyroid/throat

cardiac plexus/heart

solar plexus/stomach

adrenals/kidneys

sacral/base

91

COLOUR

THE CHARACTERISTICS OF COLOUR

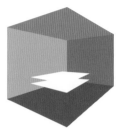

EACH COLOUR IN THE SPECTRUM has certain characteristics and the clever designer or decorator uses them to full advantage. But most colours also have historic, symbolic and even magical associations, which can vary widely according to culture. Black cats, for instance, are considered lucky in most European countries, whereas in the USA the reverse is true. Red is the colour of fertility in some Asian countries and is used for bridal gowns in India, but green represents fertility to Europeans as it did to the ancient Egyptians.

BLUE is the colour of harmony, peace and devotion but it can also be an exotic and expensive colour associated with royalty. It is usually a cool colour and the paler values in particular will create a sense of space as they bring to mind wide vistas and endless horizons.

Blue is fairly low in reflective value so will diffuse and soften bright sunlight, and calm down a very bright, sunny room. However, blue can be very cold and in the stronger, pure forms can be demanding. Use it with care in small spaces; you may need to warm it up with yellow, red or orange, especially in cold or north-facing rooms.

The greyed values of blue can be rather dull, so these need contrasting with a warm colour and a neutral such as white or cream. The blue-greens can be highly stimulating and exotic; they are associated with rare minerals such as turquoise, jade and lapis lazuli as well as peacocks' tails and dragonflies.

Individual colours can improve our health. Blue, a cool, peaceful and harmonious colour, can help to reduce stress, relieve tension and ease high blood pressure and insomnia.

lapis lazuli

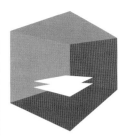

VIOLET and PURPLE also have associations with royalty (Imperial purple) but symbolically they represent sensitivity, good taste and a liking for the arts, music and philosophy. Purple is also a dignified colour, associated with age, and it was a favourite Victorian colour of mourning.

Stronger versions of purple can be vibrant and demanding, so be sure to use them with care. Team them with crisp neutrals, or create a contrast with either cool or warm pastels. Purple is cold when it is on the cool side of the colour spectrum, so treat it as you would blue; when purple goes towards

red, it becomes a much warmer colour. The paler values – mauves and lilacs – create an impression of space in a room.

Wooden panelling, natural objects and warm violets and purples make this bathroom a comfortable and relaxing environment, ideal for relieving the strains of a busy day.

A rich red colour
scheme creates a
welcoming and
nurturing atmosphere.

The temptation of a bowl of strawberries is ample proof of the ability of the colour red to stimulate appetite.

RED is the warmest advancing colour of all and is associated with vitality, energy and aggressiveness. This is also the colour of danger, which is why it is used for fire engines and 'stop' lights. Red can make people feel physically warm, so it may be a good colour to use in cold rooms.

The stronger values of red can be highly stimulating and over-powering, so use this colour with discretion. Red can make a room appear small, intimate and cosy, but can also be enclosing – even claus-trophobic. Red is also an appetite-inducing colour, which is why many restaurants are decorated in various versions of red. Consider carefully whether you would want to use red in a dining room.

When red is mixed with white it becomes softer and less intense. Traditionally, pink was associated with love and romance, although this is now disappearing. As more blue is introduced to the pink, making it mauve or lilac pink, the colour becomes more mysterious and sophisticated, useful for creating a cool, spacious ambience.

The deeper, greyed values of red – plum rose and rich burgundy – add richness, elegance and warmth, without being too over-powering. Like all warm colours, these benefit from the introduction of a little contrast by way of cool colour, or definite neutrals such as pure white, black and clear grey.

Pink is associated with love, the heart beating with passion. Valentine hearts use the symbolic colour.

A combination of cool, sophisticated mauve and pastel pink lends an adult but romantic theme to a bedroom.

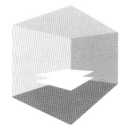

The powerful orange of the flower is invigorating and exciting, while the muted orange of the walls creates an earthy, exotic ambience.

Buddhist monks can be recognized from a distance by their bright orange robes. To Buddhists, orange symbolizes humility.

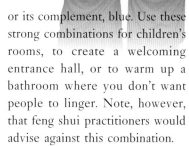

ORANGE brings together the physical energy of red and the intellect of yellow. In its pure form, it is as demanding, intense and advancing as red. Associated with strength and endurance, orange in Greek mythology was the colour attributed to Zeus, the supreme ruler of the gods.

In the East, Buddhist monks wear saffron (bright yellow/ orange) robes to symbolize their humility; in Japan, orange is the colour of love and happiness.

Orange can be used in the decoration of your home in much the same way as red. It will create a highly stimulating scheme if stronger values are used, or when it is contrasted with black, white or its complement, blue. Use these strong combinations for children's rooms, to create a welcoming entrance hall, or to warm up a bathroom where you don't want people to linger. Note, however, that feng shui practitioners would advise against this combination.

Pale orange, apricot and peach are subtle, delicate colours that give a warm and welcoming effect, and can be used in a similar way to pink. Deeper-toned oranges – terracotta, tan, chestnut – are versatile decorating colours. Working like a neutral, they can be used with both warm and cool colours. Used as the main colours with white or cream, they will create a relaxed and warm atmosphere.

You can't help but be cheered by springtime yellow flowers or a bright yellow room.

YELLOW is a joyful and uplifting colour, synonymous with summer. The symbolic colour of the life-giving sun, yellow is in tune with nature. The clear yellow of spring flowers revives our spirits after the winter months, while deep yellow-golds are associated with the harvest and fruitfulness. Yellow is also associated with creative energy, the mind, intellect and power, and symbolizes wealth. The down side of this colour is when it is associated with sickness such as jaundice and with the yellow flag of quarantine.

Almost any value of yellow will bring warmth and light into the darkest and coldest room. But bright yellow can be highly stimulating so use it with care in small spaces. Yellow can create a focal point with a neutral, or cold, contrasting background to set it off. The paler yellows have a high reflective value and will make a small, dark room look much larger, as well as lighter, especially if teamed with subtle blue.

The deeper yellows – mustard, gold and golden-bronze – are rich, warm and inviting with a subdued glow. They will help to create an elegant, sophisticated, welcoming atmosphere, and can be contrasted with a clear, neutral or a sharp, cold colour. When yellow becomes yellow/green it can become acid. Some of the deeper, greyed yellow/greens, particularly olive, may appear rich and exciting in daylight, but under artificial light they become dull and grey. This colour therefore should always be exceptionally well lit.

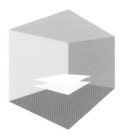

GREEN is the colour of nature – and hope! It is associated with green shoots appearing and the resurgence of nature after winter or drought. In many cultures, green is also the colour of fertility. Today, the 'green' image also sums up the current refusal to accept pollution and the spoiling of our environment – truly a healthy 'green' home.

Coming halfway between the warm and cool colours of the spectrum, green is the colour of harmony. It is easy on the eye and creates an atmosphere of relaxation. However, when green is contrasted with its complement red, the result is highly stimulating.

Green recedes, so pale values of green can be used to suggest an impression of space. This colour will also bring a verdant, fresh vibrant feel into a sunless basement, flat or town house in the 'concrete jungle' of the city, especially if mid- and deep-toned greens are combined with pale yellow. You can also use green in order to bring a feel of nature into the home.

Most greens are cool, so you might well need to warm them up with a few contrasting accessories and crisp neutrals. Some grey/greens and yellow/greens can appear to change colour at night so they need very careful lighting.

In feng shui, green is the colour of balance, harmony and peace. On the colour wheel too it sits midway between cool and warm. Green heralds the arrival of spring and hope; it can have a stabilizing effect.

Vibrant green walls and a mass of plants bring an immediate feeling of nature into this kitchen. Used in the home, green, and its varying shades, can create a fresh, relaxing atmosphere.

BLACK, WHITE and GREY

are really the non-colours, but they too have their own symbolism. Black implies the extinction of all light and colour; however, without light there is no life, so pure black is rarely found in nature. It is associated with darkness, witchcraft and evil and is almost universally the colour of death, grief, mourning and penitence. Yet, by contrast, in Western fashion, black is often seen as the height of sophistication and glamour, hence the popularity of the little black dress.

Grey is often associated with age and wisdom, as in 'grey matter' or *eminence gris*, but it also suggests shadows – pale greys can have an ethereal quality – and sometimes even dullness. Consider for example the idea of grey-faced people. Both black and grey are often linked to uniformity, bureaucracy and institutions.

White is the colour of winter and of the moon goddess. It symbolizes innocence, faith and purity and is associated with chastity and joy, which is why it is the bridal and baptismal colour in so many different cultures. White can also be seen as the colour of submission and surrender, hence the white flag of truce.

In design and decoration, apart from being a successful neutral, white is seen as the colour of health and hygiene. White is used to suggest and maintain cleanliness in kitchens, food shops, hospitals and dental and doctors' surgeries. It is also used in the same way in food-product packaging.

In fashion, black and white retain an almost timeless sophistication. In feng shui, black is powerful and represents money.

Black and white produce a very smart office space and bedroom in a converted garage. By contrast, muted grey paintwork and neutral walls are more peaceful and appropriate for a dining area.

White can be either stark or peaceful. Often associated with hygiene, it gives a dramatic and exceptionally clean feel to this very streamlined kitchen.

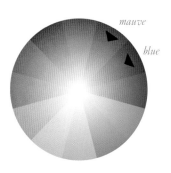

mauve

blue

Colours that are adjacent in the colour wheel are harmonious with each other and can be used together for an attractive decorative scheme.

A monochromatic colour scheme can work particularly well in bathrooms, giving a fresh, clean feel, particularly when delicate tones are chosen.

WHEN YOU ARE PLANNING a colour scheme you need to think about many things: the size and shape of the room you are going to decorate, its orientation, that is which way it faces, and how much natural daylight it receives. This in particular will have an effect on whether you choose warm or cool colours, and whether your colours should be pale, bright, rich or subtle. You also need to consider the purpose and function of the room, what you are going to use it for, as well as the basic style you are aiming to achieve. You may also need to take into account the architectural style, if any.

A modern kitchen, for example, may well be inviting, attractive, stimulating and hygienic in pure white, black and grey with touches of shiny steel and chrome, and strong primary red or orange accents, but such a combination would look out of place in a country cottage kitchen or traditional sitting room.

TONAL CONTRAST You
also need to consider the values and saturation or intensity of the colours you choose. If you put too many similar tones together, the effect will lack contrast, so you should aim to combine different tonal values. This is particularly important if you are working with a monochromatic (one-colour) scheme, or one based on neutrals (yes, neutrals also have different tonal values), or if you are going to decorate your room with mainly plain surfaces, keeping pattern to a minimum.

The secret of all successful interior design relies on combining the practical with the aesthetic. Therefore it is often wise to choose the mid- and darker tones for those surfaces which receive the most wear such as the floor and upholstery, and to use the paler colours for the ceiling, walls, woodwork and areas that are easier to wash or clean. Stronger and pure hues can be introduced in the shape of accents and accessories, or as an integral part of the design on a patterned item.

BRINGING IN HARMONY
One of the most harmonious colour schemes is made by working with different values of one colour, to create a monochromatic, or one-colour scheme. Such a scheme will also be calming and relaxing, and, if you use blues or greens, will suggest space and elegance. Again, you should aim for a practical as well as an attractive scheme, relating the strength of the colour to the surface on which it is to be used – and the wear and tear it will receive.

As you saw from the colour wheel, colours that are next or adjacent to each other naturally harmonize with each other. For example, you could create an attractive scheme based on pale primrose, deep gold, lime and holly greens, perhaps accented with turquoise (blue/green). In this way both monochromatic and adjacent schemes will be harmonious because they are based on close colour families.

A warm but contemporary feel is achieved in this sitting room by combining mellow reds and oranges with a splash of purple.

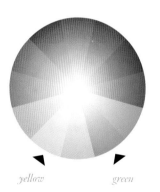

yellow   *green*

Yellow and green combine to give an elegant, harmonious charm in an imposing hallway.

orange ▶   ◀ *blue*

BRINGING IN CONTRAST

Contrasting or complementary colour schemes are the most stimulating and should be used for areas where you do not want to sit and relax. You can create contrasting schemes by using two dynamic opposites: yellow/ violet; red/green; or blue/orange, but again think about achieving tonal contrast and the use of a neutral as a link. Pale primrose combined with rich plum-purple and cream as the neutral; deep Indian red contrasted with pale apple green and sparked with white; lapis lazuli blue with terracotta and pale silver grey, are all complementary schemes. A simpler way of creating a contrasting scheme is to combine a warm with a cool colour, which need not necessarily be complete opposites, blue with yellow for example.

Contrasting colour schemes liven and stimulate a living space, but can also provide a harmonious feel. You can create contrasts by taking two dynamic opposites or by blending cool and warm colours. More complex schemes involve using three contrasting colours.

purple ▲

orange ◣

green ◢

Tricks of the trade

Whichever type of scheme you choose – whether it is based on mainly warm or mainly cool colours, a monochromatic tone or a subtle blend of neutrals – remember one of the tricks used by the professionals: add a few sharp contrasts with vases, towels, kitchenware and other accessories to emphasize and underline the effect you have created.

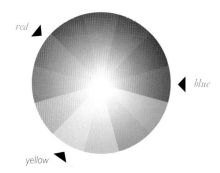

red

blue

yellow

A triad of the primary colours – red, yellow and blue – gives a colourful scheme which needs not be overpowering if the tones are carefully chosen.

THREE-COLOUR SCHEMES

It is possible to make contrasting schemes that are more complex. A triadic scheme, for example, is based on the use of three colours that are equidistant on the colour wheel. You may choose to use the primaries of red, yellow and blue to create a very stimulating scheme, which is sometimes appropriate for children's rooms. Or you could use three secondaries such as orange, green and violet; or even three of the tertiary colours such as blue/green, red/violet and yellow/orange. Again, it is not necessary to use the pure hues, as more subtle values of the colours will still create a contrast.

A split complementary scheme combines either a primary or a secondary colour with the two colours which are positioned either side of its complement, so red combined with blue/green and yellow/green; orange mated with blue/violet and blue/green; yellow with red/violet and blue/violet, and so on, are all split complementary schemes, even if different tints, tones and shades of the colours are used.

MOOD
MAKING

STYLE AND COLOUR SCHEMES APART, when you choose and use colour you are also aiming to create a particular mood or ambience. Colour in its own right creates atmosphere; pattern and texture can add an extra visual dimension and help to set the style of the room.

The moods you create with colour reflect the characteristics of the individual colours. Using colour you can create rooms that feel warm or cold, spacious or intimate, exciting or restful. The choice is yours, depending on your needs and aims.

A room decorated in a neutral/off-white scheme will have an open, airy feeling and a sense of light – even if the room is dark. Any touch of colour will be highlighted. Light-toned wood is a natural complement to cream and off-white, harmonizing without drawing focus.

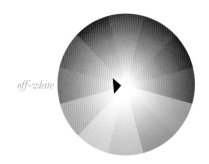

off-white

CREATING A FEELING OF SPACE
The cool colours of the spectrum work well in warm, sunny south- and west-facing rooms; giving an impression of elegance, and, in their paler values, a spacious feel. Strong, cold colours can also be uncomfortable, so may be used to prevent people from lingering in a room, especially if the cool tones are combined with a strong contrasting, warm colour.

If you prefer a calm, elegant look, opt for the cooler greens, blue/greens, blue, indigo, purple – the receding or short-wavelength colours, which seem to go away from you. These are also space makers, and will help to increase the size of an area visually, especially if you use paler values such as powder blue, mint green, silver/sage, lilac, pale green/greys.

For a spacious look too, choose a scheme based on a blue, blue/green, green, lilac or cool grey; to introduce a little warmth, work with yellow, gold and touches of brass: pink, rose and subtle red; pale peach, terracotta and copper – always within the same colour segment.

Cool, spacious schemes can sometimes lack interest. To counter this, introduce a neutral colour, and at least one colourful, contrasting accessory or accent. Think about adding a touch of Indian red, ochre, or sizzling pink to pastel blues; or subtle green, rich tones to contrast with creamy neutrals. A patterned surface too, perhaps in the form of wall coverings, flooring, curtains or upholstery fabrics, can add contrast to the main colours.

light-toned peach

CREATING A FEELING OF WARMTH

All the warm colours – in their various tints, tones and shades – will suggest a feeling of wellbeing. They work particularly well in cold, dark and north- or west-facing rooms. The warm colours can be used to create a cosy, intimate ambience, and to make a vast area, such as the entrance hall in a large, old property, seem smaller and more welcoming to visitors and to those who live there.

Use the advancing or dominant hues to achieve this intimate and warm effect. These include the warm, long wavelength colours such as red/violet; red; red/orange; orange; yellow/orange; yellow and some yellow/greens. You can also call on their various tints, tones and shades such as pink, rose, wine red, peace, gold, apricot, yellow and terracotta to create the same result.

For that added touch, you can drop strong, cool accents into a mainly warm scheme. Jade, peacock and sky blue, for instance, can be used successfully with peach or terracotta.

Warm tones like salmon and peach can make even this large space seem cosy and comfortable.

Getting the right match

Colour-matching should never be a hit and miss affair. When you are searching for the various components of your colour scheme, the only way to ensure an accurate colour match is to take samples of existing items with you. If you are looking for colour to match existing floor, walls, curtains or furniture, take a sample of the carpet or other fabric with you, bearing in mind that it may have faded through time. You can also take pieces of coloured paper, woods, embroidery silks or ribbon.

Don't match to photographs or leaflets because colour printing is rarely accurate. Instead, ask suppliers or retailers for fabric, flooring, or wallpaper samples, as large as possible, and take them home so that you can look at them against the original items in both day and night lighting.

With paint or stain for walls, woodwork, floor and ceiling, buy a small amount, if little tester pots are unavailable, and paint it onto lining paper or a spare piece of wood. Try to do as large a sample as possible to get a realistic picture.

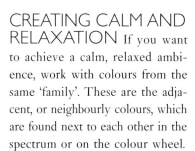

mauve

yellow

You can create an exciting colour scheme for a child's bedroom by combining contrasting colours, such as purple and yellow. If the effect is too dramatic, soften it with subtler values of the same colours.

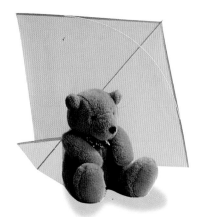

CREATING EXCITEMENT

The way you put colours together is called creating colour harmonies, although sometimes you may be wanting to create excitement rather than harmony. For instance, if you want to achieve a stimulating effect, perhaps in a children's playroom or in a room, such as the bathroom, where you want people to move on, use contrasting or complementary colours.

Try combining a warm with a cool colour, such as red with green, blue with orange, purple and yellow. These are all direct opposites on the colour wheel, and can be very strong and dominant.

You can create a softer but still stimulating scheme by using pale and subtle values of the complementary colours, or by teaming yellow and blue; grey and pink.

It is a good idea to add plenty of textural contrast to exciting, stimulating schemes. To do this, combine shiny, light-reflecting surfaces with rough, rustic and matt, light-absorbing ones. Also try to introduce some delicate, light-diffusing effects such as sheer fabrics, lace panels, slatted blinds, cane and wickerwork.

CREATING CALM AND RELAXATION

If you want to achieve a calm, relaxed ambience, work with colours from the same 'family'. These are the adjacent, or neighbourly colours, which are found next to each other in the spectrum or on the colour wheel.

To create a sense of calm, try working with yellow/green; green/blue and green. Alternatively, you could work up a scheme with rose, lilac, lavender and blue, or introduce more warmth using yellow with yellow/orange, tans and terracotta.

Calm schemes such as these may include mainly warm or mainly cool colours; this will depend on which segment of the colour wheel you choose. They may even be a combination of both, in which case the scheme would become more stimulating.

For an even more relaxing theme, work up a monochromatic colour scheme. This type of harmony is based on different values of one basic hue, so you need to work within only one segment of the colour wheel and to achieve plenty of tonal contrast in order to ensure the effect is not too bland.

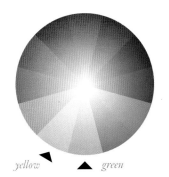

Opposing colours stimulate and excite; adjacent colours are calmer and more relaxing.

yellow ▲ ▲ *green*

USING NEUTRALS

You can also use neutrals and natural textures to create a relaxing area, but make sure they come from the same colour 'family'. The only true neutrals are black, white and grey (made by mixing white together in different proportions to create different values), but these three non-colours used together can be highly stimulating, especially if combined with bold patterns and lots of different textures.

These days there are other 'accepted' neutrals even though some may have a different colour bias. They include cream, beige, off-white, taupe, mushroom, brown and the colours of natural, untreated materials, such as wood, sisal, hemp, seagrass, jute, slate, clay, undyed canvas, linen, cotton and muslin.

There are also different 'natural whites', usually created by taking a large amount of white, very pale grey or cream, and adding a small amount of colour. The result is usually a rather wishy-washy version of the original colour, which looks almost like white. The colour will, in reality, be blueish, greenish, pinkish or even yellow-toned, and needs very careful colour-matching, because the original colour becomes more obvious when seen in relation to other colours in the scheme.

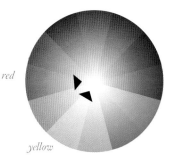

red

▲ ▲

yellow

Depending on its shade, blue can produce a cool, stylish atmosphere, although darker values can be vibrant. More neutral colours, such as beige, cream or mushroom used with natural materials, help to create a calm, relaxed room.

ADDING
A THIRD
DIMENSION

You can create bold patterns by grouping floor tiles in zig zags and introducing furniture in contrasting shapes. But confine them to less-used areas.

Too much pattern in a kitchen can be tiring. Limit it to chequered floor tiles, with objects and furniture creating interest.

A SUCCESSFUL ROOM scheme includes not only colour but also an effective use of pattern combined with textural and tonal contrasts. Like colour, patterns can help to create calm feelings, or they can excite you, or entice you, drawing you into a room. Patterns can also appear to change the proportions of a space, and suggest a modern or period flavour.

Bold patterns work like warm colours; they tend to advance, so appear to be coming towards you. They give a room a stimulating and exciting feel. They should be used with care and work best in large, cold spaces or on large surfaces. Small patterns are like cool, pale colours; they seem to recede and go away from you. They will create an impression of space but very small mini-print patterns tend to fade into insignificance if used over a large area. To avoid this happening, you may prefer to opt for an interesting texture rather than a design.

The use of pattern can also help to set a specific style, either a period flavour or more modern ambience. The right choice of pattern and colour can enhance and echo the original architectural style. It can emphasize important features or bring character and presence into what might otherwise be a rather bland space.

But what exactly is pattern? It can be a linear design, printed or hand-applied on fabrics, wall-coverings, floorings, or ceramic tiles, or a design woven into fabrics, stencilled onto walls, furniture or woodwork, added onto ceilings with decorative plasterwork – even furniture can suggest pattern.

Patterns can also be made by grouping together several objects or similar items. Individual floor or wall tiles, for example, may be plain individually but can be grouped together to create a pattern. Grouped tiles, for instance, can create bold and geometric patterns, especially if different or contrasting colours are used or if some tiles are cut into triangles or light and dark tiles laid in a distinctive chequerboard pattern.

An arrangement of various objects, pictures grouped on a wall, a miscellany of cushions thrown onto a sofa or bed can also create patterns, provided they are made of contrasting colours and forms. Such patterning is flexible because you can change or alter it as you wish. It can also be calmer and more harmonious than the use of bold design.

Like colour, pattern falls into two main types: those which 'advance' or stimulate, and those which 'recede' and create a calming influence. 'Neutral' patterns can be used to make visual links between patterned surfaces, or on their own. These include the checks, stripes, plaids, mini-prints and 'quiet' geometrics, which are often timeless.

When choosing a pattern, think about its design and scale, and the surface on which you will use it. Heavily patterned walls and bold carpet designs can be dominant. Patterned curtains, which hang in folds, can be more flexible and fluid, and create interesting designs when the curtains are drawn. Patterned curtains against plain walls can be effective, as can a bold plain colour against patterned walls. If you prefer your windows to blend in with the rest of the decor, choose curtains that co-ordinate with the wall coverings.

TAKING CARE There are certain areas in a home where it is not wise to use too strong a pattern – on kitchen work surfaces for example, where they can cause eye strain. Wall tiles in bathrooms and kitchens need careful selection – too bold a pattern will become irritating but tiles are difficult to remove if you change your mind.

Walls are another surface where too bold a design can become difficult to live with and, as walls are often not completely square, the pattern can appear to be slipping off the wall. Always look at wall coverings unwrapped, and with at least two widths side-by-side to assess the overall effect. Floor tiles should be seen in a mirrored box, which suggests a whole floor. A very bold design on a carpet, particularly in the hall, stairs, landing and main rooms of a home can seem to come up at you every time you open the door!

Pattern through time

Incorporating pattern into a decorating scheme always needs careful consideration and its use has changed considerably over the centuries. During the Georgian era pattern was usually restricted to fabrics, carpets or created by the use of decorative plasterwork and grouping of patterned china, but in Regency times pattern was provided by wallpaper panels as well as on fabrics. The early and mid-Victorians specialized in a riot of pattern. As a backlash, the Arts and Crafts movement preferred plainer surfaces, with the pattern interest added in fabrics, rugs and furniture. During the 1920s, plain walls and floors were popular, until the geometric and specific styles of Art Deco were woven into rugs, and printed on fabrics. The Bauhaus influence and the minimalist look of the 1930s, succeeded by the hi-tech style of the 1950s, relied more on texture and colour although bold geometric patterns were used for wallpapers and fabrics. Most recently, a well-balanced scheme has usually consisted of two, or at the most three, patterned surfaces, although the vogue for co-ordinated and companion ranges has made it possible to use the same pattern – or the positive and negative of the same design – on several items from wallcoverings through to flooring.

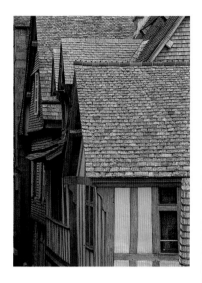

The use of local building materials and traditional architectural styles dictates the colour schemes and appearance of these French houses.

This French country house blends perfectly with its surroundings; insensitive modernization would completely ruin its appearance.

THE TRADITION of painting our houses, both inside and out, goes back into the mists of time, to when early peoples painted the walls of their caves. But as archaeologists have proved, early forms of architecture, such as Aztec pyramids, were either faced with metal and ceramics, or covered in painted frescoes. This made them stand out as 'important' buildings but frequently the colours chosen were also highly symbolic.

Temples, palaces and other buildings in ancient Egypt and Greece were often brightly painted – the Parthenon (432BC) was painted in bright red, blue and pink, with gilding applied to the friezes above the white limewashed columns that may have symbolized virginity.

At the height of the Art Deco period in Britain, Europe and the USA – which took much of its inspiration from Egypt after the discovery of Tutankhamen's tomb in 1922 – this look was copied. Buildings by Gaudi in Spain, for example, were often clad in colourful ceramics and the famous Hoover factory in Middlesex, England, which was built in

the 1930s, is a combination of white and bright reds, blues, greens and gold – a 'temple' in essence to the vacuum cleaner.

But colour is not only used for public buildings – paint and various colour washes have been used for centuries to decorate and protect the walls and timbers of our houses.

Historically, villages, towns and cities were built from local materials and, until the end of the 18th century, were painted with pigments made from local deposits of earth. The colours depended on geographical location: rich ochre yellow and terracotta colours are typical of certain regions in France and 'Suffolk Pink' is a strong colour relating to the clay present in Britain's Suffolk soil.

When planning colours for the exterior of your home, particularly the façade, try to choose a scheme which will be in harmony with the environment. In a rural environment, you could collect and analyse local soil samples and collect examples of the predominant building materials. Check these against an exterior paint chart – you will find several manufacturers have produced ranges which are sympathetic to the various regional colours.

In the country, local stone, flint or slate might be used for the main construction. When local brick kilns were established, the bricks would have been used locally and would therefore be in keeping with the environment. It was only when bricks started to be transported – by canal and then by rail – that

American
plantation-style
houses were built
in such a way that
they created a cool
refreshing
environment to
withstand the
southern heat.

House styles and
colours should echo
their environment.
This old Suffolk
cottage has been
painted a candy pink
in keeping with
regional tradition.

Contrasting primary
colours harmonize
well in a hot, sunny
climate but would be
unsuitable for colder,
northern regions.

brick buildings became out of tune
with their surroundings. Some farm
buildings were painted with local
pigments for the purpose of camou-
flaging them, so they would fade
into the surrounding background
or earth.

Today it is not wise to clad a
building with something which is
out of keeping with the houses in
the surrounding area. In a simple
brick-built terrace for example, a
faux stone façade stands out like a
sore thumb, as does any other
example of over-improving, which
includes   many   replacement
windows (and bulls' eye panes);
over-ornate front doors, fences and

gates; false beams; phoney plastic
pillars, columns and porticoes. On
the other hand, any original
architectural detail should be pre-
served and enhanced wherever this
is possible.

There is no reason why simple
houses should not be painted in
attractive colours. In Italy, Greece,
the South of France, Spain, Mexico
and Portugal the exteriors are often
colourfully painted or clad with
ceramics. Of course, these are seen
under strong, bright sunlight most
of the time, and against a pure blue
sky. In northern cities, strong, clear
colours can sometimes appear
too brash.

Care should be taken not to
create a scheme which would clash
with the surrounding houses. The
combination of colours for the
façade, woodwork, rainwater pipes
and gutters, eaves, front gate and
fence or railings needs to be
worked out as carefully as a colour
scheme for a room would be. It is
possible to use colour outside to
improve the proportions of a building visually. For example a tall
narrow house can be made to look
wider and a small, squat building
can be made to appear taller than
it really is.

111

COLOUR

SCENTS

AND SOUND

Once you have planned your home to function efficiently, banished all clutter, chosen suitable colour schemes and sorted out the lighting, it is time to spoil yourself. A healthy home should be somewhere to relax, enjoy your surroundings and pamper yourself. So if you have always wanted to sleep in silk sheets, surround your bath with scented candles, or play and sing along with your preferred type of music – go for it.

Pleasing sounds encourage relaxation – the natural sounds of bird song and flowing water, the tinkling of strategically placed wind chimes, even recorded sounds of waves, are soothing and smooth away stress which has accumulated during the day. Playing a musical instrument can be very therapeutic, and, if you don't play an instrument, make time to listen to your favourite music and relax. Silence too is essential for physical and emotional health – a house full of jarring, continuous noise is not conducive to relaxation.

Clean, pure air flowing through the home encourages health. Make sure the air in your home is not polluted, check humidity, temperature levels and ventilation. A moving flow of air can refresh in summer but be too chilling in winter. You may want to consider air conditioning, or ionizers and humidifiers to purify the air if anyone in the family has breathing problems.

You can enhance air quality and atmosphere in your home with scented candles, oils, sweet-smelling flowers and herbs and pot pourri, but always use natural products. Consider drying your own herbs; their scent adds pleasure to the home and many have specific health-giving qualities.

Think about how you want your home to feel. Touch is an important sensation; the textures you use in your home can make it more sensuous – velvet or silk drapes, satin sheets, shaggy pile rugs, chenille upholstery, fur fabric cushions are all eminently 'strokeable'. Juxtapose them with metallic or light-filtering textiles to provide tactile and visual contrast. The patina of beautifully polished furniture is both pleasing to the eye and wonderful to touch.

Use natural materials in your home – pure cotton sheets, muslin and voile drapes, lace covers on bedside tables, cotton curtains and natural woods.

Water too creates a soothing or sensuous sybaritic mood. Use it in the garden, on a patio or create water features inside. Whirlpool, massage baths and showers ease muscular pains and sooth away stress and tension. A long hot soak in a bath, filled with scented water, and lit by candlelight, with your favourite drink close to hand, can be the height of pleasure. You might even like to install a sauna for deep cleanliness.

REDUCING NOISE

N<small>O HOUSE CAN EVER</small> be totally silent; without some sounds it would lack life and be almost sepulchral. But quietness and peace are essential for relaxation and health. A noisy house is not a relaxing one and it may be necessary to sort out adequate sound insulation for your home.

Noise – or unwanted sound – bombards us constantly and can have a very negative effect on our health, causing irritation, stress and even physical ailments. Some noise penetrates the home from outside, perhaps from nearby roads, schools, car parks, airports or railways. If you live in an apartment, terraced or semi-detached house, you may also experience noise from neighbours – remember that your noise can be equally distracting to them.

Families can create their own noise pollution, shouting, arguing and playing music without regard to others. Today most modern homes too are filled with noise–generating technology – answer phones and early morning alarms bleep at us; dishwashers and washing machines can be extremely intrusive, particularly when they reach their 'spin' cycle; telephones and televisions can be intolerable; and vacuum cleaners cause an unpleasant drone.

For the sake of a healthy home, you will need some form of noise control to prevent unwanted sounds travelling up and down through floors, ceilings and walls. Whole-house planning is a sensible start to cutting down on noise problems, allocating rooms, or using them, according to their noise impact. For instance, avoid putting heavy-footed, music-playing teenagers above their grandmother's bedroom, the main bedroom, or next to a nursery. If space allows, you may even be able to create a separate music room, perhaps in the garage, although realistically most of us live in fairly small properties; we rarely have enough room to provide special facilities and have to work with what we have.

NOISE INSULATION

Noise travels through floorboards and along floor joists so a thick layer of insulation between joists, floor and ceiling below will help to deaden sound. Carpet or carpet tiles also absorb noise, especially if they are laid over a dense underlay. If carpet is not a practical choice, because of hygiene or if family members suffer from allergies, choose a quiet-inducing surface underfoot. Cork, rubber or linoleum – even cushioned vinyl – will be 'bouncier' and less noisy than wood, ceramic tiles, slate and other hard floorings, but for good feng shui, you should avoid artificial materials. Floorings such as wood or slate are natural materials and can be softened with rugs to muffle sound further; make sure they have non-slip backings or use washable cotton rugs.

Noise also passes through house walls, especially if they are solidly constructed, which transmit sound efficiently. To reduce the amount of sound, you can effectively insulate the wall by creating a second layer and leaving a space between that and the wall. You can line walls with wood, perhaps using tongue and groove in a country-style kitchen or bathroom, or laminated panels, particularly in a modern bathroom. You can also use special insulated compressed fibreboard to clad walls, and then decorate over them, either using lining paper and paint, or wallpaper. As all these are battened onto the original wall, you can leave as much space between the two layers as practical. You can also muffle sound by placing insulating board behind cupboards or wardrobes. Of course, wardrobes full of clothes make a natural sound barrier.

Consider using equipment at a time when it would be less offensive to the ear.

Perceived decibels	Typical sounds
140–130	Jet engine at 30m (100ft); pneumatic riveter; hydraulic press at 1m (39in)
120	**Threshold of pain** 1 billion times greater than the least audible sound; loud thunder
110	Discotheque speakers at 1.2m (4ft); pneumatic drill
100	Food blender at 61cm (24in); nearby chain saw or motor cycle
90	Heavy truck; automatic lathe
80	**Danger level** inside small car; noisy office; alarm clock; window air conditioner
70	Busy shopping street; large department store; building noise; vacuum cleaner, food mixer, washing machine
60	Normal conversation at 1m (39in)
50	Quiet street; inside average home
40	Quiet office; quiet conversation, residential area at night; refrigerator
30	Ticking watch; rustle of paper; whispered conversation; bedroom
20	Quiet country lane
10	Leaves rustling in wind
0	**Threshold of hearing**

Living on a busy road or at a frequently backed-up intersection can be stressful because of noise. Proper insulation and careful decorating can protect your ears and peace of mind.

NOISE CONTROL

Thick curtains at an outside window provide two types of insulation – against cold draughts and noise. They also prevent indoor noise from disturbing those outside!

A window shade can enhance the insulating properties of curtains. Four-poster beds with full curtains have been used for centuries to keep out the cold.

FABRIC SOLUTIONS
Fabric also softens sound. Fabric-covered walls therefore act as sound barriers and are also decorative. Fabric is usually fixed to walls by stretching it over battens, or attaching it to a special track. The fabric is slipped into place between two flanges, and can be pleated into position for an elegant appearance.

Uncovered windows let in sound as well as cold. Heavy, lined curtains provide good insulation against both; they absorb sound and guard against draughts. They also prevent heat and noise escaping from the window. If floor-to-ceiling and possibly wall-to-wall drapes are used, combined with blinds close to the glass, this will act as an extra insulatory layer.

If you have a severe noise, and possibly weather, problem, you will need to consider double – or even triple glazing for windows. For this to be fully effective, you should have a gap of at least 10cm/4in (ideally 15–20cm/6–8in) between the layers of glass. Laminated glass is a good idea in conservatories, glazed rear and entrance doors, particularly for safety if there are children in the house, and also if burglaries are a possibility.

A ceiling, lavishly tented with fabric is exotic and alluring and will help to deaden sound. A canopy above a bed, with side drapes, has the same attractions – it is exotic and reduces unwanted noise. Interestingly, the original four-poster bed was designed for such purposes – to keep out draughts, make bedfellows warm and cosy and to deaden sound

Soft, thick floor
coverings, such as
cork, sisal or
carpeting, can
greatly decrease the
noise of creaking
floorboards or
heavy footfalls.

from outside, and inside, the bed drapes. When this type of bed was originally invented there was rarely a separate bed chamber, and the bed was positioned on an upper gallery of a 'hall house' – usually one giant room with a fire in the centre, a hole in the roof for smoke and an upper gallery for a little privacy – and minstrels. Today, feng shui practitioners recommend a canopy and side drapes or four-poster bed for those having difficulty relaxing and switching off from the stresses of the day.

Hard-textured surfaces such as ceramic tiled walls and floors, slate, quarry tiles, marble, wood, laminated, granite and steel work tops all reflect sound and increase decibel levels – as a result kitchens and bathrooms are often the noisiest rooms in the house, apart from teenage bedrooms. You can offset this by adding soft textures – large, fluffy, washable cotton rugs to a bathroom and a square of rush matting or sisal to the kitchen floor, or use cork, rubber, or cushioned vinyl as hygienic and softer alternatives to hard flooring.

You could also consider a 'floating floor'; this consists of a floor surface that rests on a resilient pad positioned above the main structural floor. Cork or laminate floorings are often best laid in this way. Adding an enclosed porch to the front entrance or to the back door will also cut down on any noise and draughts.

And if you have a balcony that you rarely use because of outside noise, you could glaze it to reduce external noise, and to make a place for green plants.

CONSIDERING OTHERS

Finally, environmental harmony is also about considering others and their health needs, and reducing any noise pollution that you may produce. As a good neighbour, you should not carry out structural or do-it-yourself work early in the morning or late at night. If you have builders working for you, discuss this with them, and ensure that they keep radios to an acceptable level, and warn immediate neighbours of any building work, or late-night parties. Work towards harmony with your neighbours by using your household appliances during the day rather than at night, not plumbing them into party walls or by insulating the wall behind them, and keep doors shut to prevent unwanted sounds from escaping.

Practical tips
• Save any spare carpet or carpet tiles and place them, in layers, underneath the television, radio, music system or keyboard to absorb sound.
• If you are replacing windows, make sure they are adequately insulated from noise as well as cold and draughts.

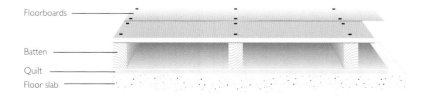

Floorboards
Batten
Quilt
Floor slab

A floating floor, created by placing floorpads between the floorboards and the structural floor, is an effective way of reducing noise.

USING SOUND CREATIVELY

Once you have removed unwanted noise, you can introduce pleasing sounds, such as a ticking clock, or running water into the garden. According to feng shui, metal wind chimes hung above the front door purify the atmosphere.

INTRODUCING SOUND into the home can stimulate, soothe, relax, reduce stress and tension and calm frayed nerves. You can use natural or human-made sounds, from the tinkling of spray water splashing over pebbles to the melodious sound of the harp or cello or the human voice reading a story or crooning a lullaby. Other sounds too can be comforting – a clock ticking or chiming, doves cooing or a cat purring.

There are many recordings and tapes available of natural sounds, which you can choose to suit your mood and the ambience of a room. The sounds of the sea and waves ebbing and flowing across the shale, a babbling brook or the crisper sound of a splashing fountain can be effective and invigorating in the bathroom or shower, or more relaxing in a conservatory. Birdsong is a far better and more stimulating noise to wake up to than the strident notes of an alarm clock; soothing birdsong is a welcoming sound in a dining room, or in the garden for meals eaten *alfresco* on the patio. Relaxing sounds are also appropriate in the bedroom and will help to prepare you for a good night's sleep.

CHIMING SOUNDS
Sound vibrates the air, stimulating the flow of chi energy and for this reason plays an important part in feng shui. For good feng shui you can use specific sounds to stimulate or cleanse the energy in areas such as dark corners, under sloping roofs, in halls and corridors and to prevent

energy stagnation. Use wind chimes, bells and clocks to create a pleasant background but place them with care so the noise they make is attractive to your ears.

Wind chimes are made from several different materials – metal, wood or ceramic. Metal chimes tend to sound clear and slightly mysterious, like a hidden flute player; ceramic chimes are more brittle; and wooden or bamboo chimes can create a softer sound, although some may appear dull and muffled. Decide where in the house and/or garden you want to site your chimes, then choose the most suitable material by checking the direction from the centre of the house. For good feng shui, metal chimes are best sited in the garden. If hung near the entrance, where noise pollution may be a problem, they help to alter the vibrations coming into the home.

Bells and gongs can be used to clear any stagnant or heavy areas of energy in the house and to stimulate the chi energy. A gong, hung in the hall near the centre of the home, will reverberate throughout the whole house when struck, which is why they have been traditionally used to summon family or guests to meals. Choose one with a deep melodious tone.

Bells can be rung by hand in any area where you want to enhance the flow of chi energy. Door bells, non-electric, can also stimulate and help to keep the chi energy force fresh and clear. Avoid door bells that play a tune.

The regularity of a ticking and chiming clock will help to create a more ordered chi energy and may help you to lead a more orderly life – the ticking broken by the occasional chime will be more stimulating and will clear chi energy periodically.

OUTDOOR SOUNDS

Plants can also help to absorb sounds; their placing is an integral part of feng shui, so they must be placed in appropriate positions. Some plants make an attractive noise – the rustling of leaves on broad-leafed trees, the sound of the wind in a border of grasses or bamboo, even reeds if you have a water feature – will all sound pleasingly natural. Such sounds will be more obvious in the garden, unless your windows are wide open, but avoid planting large trees or tall grasses too close to the house. A small sapling soon becomes a large tree, which can cut daylight. Spreading roots may also interfere with drains or the foundations, so check their final height before planting.

And of course, if you plant flowers, trees and shrubs which attract birds and insects, the happy, hazy drone of bees in spring and summer, and the birds' dawn chorus will percolate into your home. If you are incredibly lucky, a nightingale may even serenade you in the evening, something that you could record to replay in the winter months. If appropriate, you could also install a dovecote but remember that doves can cause damage to mortar in brick-built chimneys, and the pointing between courses of bricks.

Many of us have fairly stressed lives that can damage our health. Listening to outdoor sounds such as the cooing of doves or the rustling of bamboo provides much-needed calm and an important link with the natural world.

IF AS A FAMILY you enjoy making music and playing various musical instruments, there is no greater way of relaxing than to create your own harmonies. A well-tuned grand piano, a string quartet, the melodious sounds of the 'cello and harp, the silvery tones of a flute will all give immense pleasure and enjoyment to both listeners and participants. And there is no reason why family music-making should be confined to the more classical approach – you can play jazz, rock or any other type of music that turns you on. But again, consider the neighbours and insulate them from unwanted noise.

SOUND SYSTEMS Most
homes today contain music systems for playing music, relaxation tapes, and so on. Constant music can be irritating for others, so make sure your system is flexible, with effective volume control. As with any

Forget your daily cares for an hour and lose yourself in music, but consider other people in the home and do not play it too loudly or, alternatively, use a set of earphones.

Speakers placed to form a triangle

other appliances, do not place a music system too close to a party wall, or directly onto a hard floor. Stand it on an insulated surface, so that sound is contained in one area.

If you want all-round sound, you will need to site your speakers carefully. If you are buying a very sophisticated system, the supplier will advise on installation and, if your home is designed and decorated in a particular period style, you may prefer to conceal the speakers in the ceiling, in built-in furniture, or behind a pelmet or baffle. If you are setting up the system in the bedroom, speakers could be built into the bedhead, concealed behind it, or positioned in top cupboards above wardrobes.

If you have to wall- or floor-mount speakers, try to screen them in some way; use plants to camouflage floor-mounted speakers; wall-mounted speakers could be an integral part of a storage wall, where they will fade into the background. In a modern, hi-tech or minimalist setting, placing the

music system and speakers on three wheeled trolleys can provide a flexible, smart arrangement.

For good listening, place your speakers equidistant from the area where you are most likely to sit, or recline, so that you form a triangle, with your seating at the apex. The length of the sides of the triangle should be at least 2 metres, but should relate to the size of the longest wall in the room.

You can have a conveniently positioned music deck as the 'nerve centre' of your music system,

relaying music to all parts of the house, and garden, via concealed cabling and strategically positioned speakers. It can be very pleasant to listen to music while in the bath or relaxing in the bedroom; music can be an energizing addition to the kitchen when you are cooking; and a pleasing background sound when entertaining in the dining room. The type of music you choose at any time will reflect the mood and atmosphere you are hoping to create.

Again, unless your home is a detached property in its own grounds you will need to consider noise pollution and the neighbours, and ensure your house is well insulated for outgoing sounds. Keep a firm hand on the volume control button, especially if teenagers are using the system!

You can use timers to pre-set a radio, music system and lighting to come on after dark – a good security device.

Nothing sets the mood like music. Your music stereo, whether it is a small portable or an expensive sound system, can create the relaxing atmosphere that you need.

THE SOUND
OF WATER

WATER IS ESSENTIAL for life and health. The sound of moving water in and around the home encourages relaxation, meditation and wellbeing. Water has also long been used as a design feature.

Outside the home, water features with water flowing from a fountain, gushing from a gargoyle's mouth, or trickling over pebbles from level to level, will all make your garden a more relaxing place. Swimming pools too can be a source of great enjoyment, although remember that they can be noise pollutants in their own right. Their hard surfaces create a natural echo chamber and the shrieks of children or evening swimmers can annoy neighbours. Build changing areas or a filtration house to create a sound barrier; use evergreen trees planted near a pool for the same purpose.

You may choose to introduce water features indoors. These will be particularly effective in a home in the heart of the city, where there may be no access to a garden. A fountain or water sculpture will enhance a conservatory or entrance hall; it could be equally effective in the dining or sitting room, even the bedroom or study. You may also be able to install a water feature on a balcony or roof terrace, surrounded by moisture-loving plants. The noise of constantly running water can be irritating, so make sure the water can be turned off easily.

As with any decorative feature, think about enhancing a water feature with good lighting; the light catching the drops of water gushing from a fountain will look like an expensive chandelier – you might even get a rainbow as a bonus. A fish tank too can provide a water feature, and is calming in its own right.

Water sustains life and its healing qualities are well known. In your home, the gentle sound of water trickling from one level to another is a soothing sound.

Water is significant in feng shui because it activates chi. Ideally, it should flow downwards, possibly over pebbles, to move energy more easily. It should also flow towards, not away, from your home. Still water can become stagnant so change it regularly.

WATER AND FENG SHUI

Water plays an important role in feng shui. It is a powerful activator of the chi energy force and also has a special significance for health. By adding water features to house and garden you will bring in fresh energy. The water feature can be any of those discussed above but even a bird bath or bowl of clean water can improve the atmosphere and energy. The water must always be fresh and unpolluted, so will need to be changed regularly, or refilled once a day.

A waterfall, with the water falling downwards rather than gushing upwards from a fountain, will be more calming, and water flowing over pebbles, or along the bed of a stream, circumnavigating stones, statuary and other features will move chi energy more easily. The sounds will be particularly soothing, and can help you through 'rocky' stages in your life. Any fountain or water feature can also help to protect you from fast-moving energy generated by a busy road, or from the cutting chi caused by the sharp corners of another building, but it must be positioned between the heart of the home and the source of bad chi. You should aim to place water features in such a way that they balance the five elements.

A garden pond should be circular, kidney-shaped or curved in some way. Avoid sharp corners and angles, plant the pond with special plants to increase oxygenation, and introduce frogs, fish, and other aquatic animals to maintain a good ecological balance. Constantly moving water incorporated into the pond via a fountain or some other source will help to keep the water fresh and clean and will prevent stagnation.

For good feng shui, swimming pools too need careful shaping and siting. Again, use circular, curved or kidney shapes. If a rectangular or square shape is unavoidable, soften the shape with rounded corners. It should be sited in the most favourable direction – east or south-east from the centre of the home – but you also need to consider the amount of sun and shade the pool will receive. Try not to position it too close to the house walls or immediately opposite a door leading into your home. If you build an indoor pool, this should be sited in the east or south-east of your home, and it should be well ventilated so damp and condensation will not cause stagnation in the pool area, and in the rest of the house. Definitely divide the pool off from the rest of the house, and keep dividers and doors firmly closed.

In your garden, moving water should flow towards, not away from your front door, ideally flowing towards it in gentle curves – if water flows away it can take prosperity from the home.

Design and architecture have incorporated water for centuries. Water features as dramatic as this are most likely to feature in public buildings but, for good feng shui, you can incorporate a more modest fountain into your home.

Sharp edges cause cutting chi. For good feng shui, ponds, pools and other water features must be rounded, kidney-shaped or curved.

IMPROVING AIR QUALITY

Sweet-smelling country air floods into a house, blowing away the cobwebs and getting the air circulating. Rectangular window shapes bring in the good luck chi.

CLEAN, FRESH AIR flowing through your home is important to health. One of the best ways of letting fresh air into the home – and circulating it – is to ventilate the home naturally by opening windows, especially on crisp, sunny and windy days. Our grandmothers used to open bedroom windows every morning to 'air' the room and hang bedding out of the window – a traditional and thrifty custom that's well worth revising.

But many homes today are virtually sealed units. Opening the window for adequate airing or ventilation is not always feasible and much double or triple glazing is not designed for opening, although, if you are installing double glazing, try to ensure that some windows can be opened. The outside air too may be polluted, so you need to concentrate on ensuring a pure air quality within your home.

Poor or polluted air in the home can cause colds, headaches, ear, nose and throat infections,

An ionizer can help to alleviate allergies by reducing the amount of impurities in the air.

If a room does not have a window, use an extractor fan to preserve air quality.

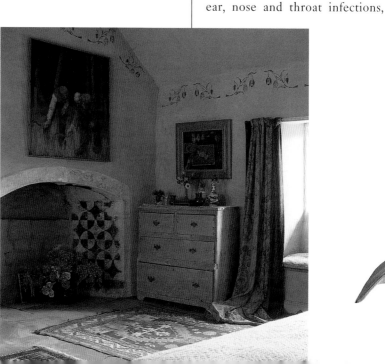

Re-opening an old fireplace may give your house an alternative form of ventilation and allow it to breathe.

asthma or allergic reactions. These can be intensified if you undertake large-scale redecoration and structural alterations, which stir up dust and other pollutants.

If you or any of your family are suffering from poor air quality, you can have the air in your home tested professionally by various organizations who will advise on appropriate health measures.

You can also take some simple precautions. If yours is an old house, which originally had an open fireplace and chimneys, and these have been sealed up, you can

You can test the humidity in your home with a special instrument called an hydrometer. The ideal humidity for a healthy home is 50–55 per cent, that is of moisture in the air. (By contrast, humidity in a desert is 20–25 per cent; in a tropical rain forest as much as 95 per cent.)

A house plant will renew oxygen levels in the air.

improve air circulation by re-opening the fireplace and the chimney, putting a cowl on the top to prevent down-draughts.

You can test for humidity and air purity yourself and then introduce purifiers and humidifiers as needed. If the air in your home is too dry, you will need a humidifier to introduce some moisture. Non-electric versions can be hung over a radiator and should be filled daily with water; you can add scented aromatherapy oil to enhance the effect. Electric versions produce steam; ultrasonic versions produce a cold vapour; fan-assisted versions can be used in large areas but do produce an annoying noise.

Excessive moisture shows itself in condensation on the inside of windows, water on sills, peeling wallpaper and mould. If damp is a problem, invest in a de-humidifier. These run on electricity and extract moisture from the atmosphere; some models are combined with a built-in heater.

If pollutants are a problem, you obviously need to try and remove pollutants but you can also use air purifiers in the home or an ionizer, which will suck up tobacco smoke, cooking smells or traffic fumes, pollens, house dust mites and so on. An ionizer does not have a filter, so is less efficient than air purifiers, which trap pollutants in an internal filter.

Hoods placed over a cooker absorb cooking smells. Some contain a carbon liner which has to be changed regularly, others

are fan-assisted but these are often noisy and can create draughts. Extractor fans fitted into an outside wall or a window, which can be either electrically or hand operated, are another, simple means of circulating purer air within the home. Air bricks too are another traditional form of ventilation.

House plants can also help to improve the environment by increasing oxygen in the atmosphere, acting as humidifiers and even filtering the air. The popular spider plant, for instance, actually removes formaldehyde and other pollutants from the atmosphere.

AIR CONDITIONING
An increasing number of homes and public buildings are being fitted with air-conditioning systems. These control both temperature and humidity and have a very positive role to play. But they can contribute to what is known as sick building syndrome, causing cold-like symptoms and breathing difficulties, most particularly when humidity levels are imbalanced. If installing air conditioning, ensure that it can both humidify and rehumidify, adding moisture back into the air to prevent it from becoming too dry. Make sure too that there is adequate ventilation so that the system circulates fresh rather than stale air. If installing a wet air-conditioning system, a closed system which uses water as a coolant, have it professionally cleaned and monitored regularly to avoid water becoming polluted with harmful bacteria or viruses.

SCENTS
FOR
HEALTH

The aromas present in your home establish a welcoming or an uncomfortable atmosphere. Strong foods, such as cabbage, garlic and fish, or tobacco smoke, can produce unpleasant and overwhelming odours.

ESTATE AGENTS TELL us if a good, appetising smell assails our nostrils the moment the front door is opened, it is one of the surest ways of attracting a would-be buyer. The smell of freshly baking bread or cakes, home-made soup or hot, brewing coffee all suggest a real comfortable home with the kitchen at its centre. But some food and other smells are an obvious turn-off – kippers, cauliflower, a smoking chip pan and, of course, stale tobacco fumes.

How your home smells will affect how comfortable you feel in your home and how welcoming it is for you and others. The sense of smell is controlled by a primitive part of the brain, which is closely connected to the area that also controls mood, emotion and personality. It also plays a key role in sexual attraction. But these days our sense of smell is becoming eroded, partly because we are forced to inhale

The aromas of bread baking and freshly brewed coffee make any environment seem homely.

Long, heavy curtains can act like a trap, holding onto dust particles, cigarette smoke and cooking smells.

Many household cleaning products have toxic fumes and should be used with care in a ventilated area.

Essential oils are distilled from flowers, woods and herbs. Heated, they subtly perfume a room.

many unpleasant and toxic smells, such as traffic fumes, plastics, paint solvents or tobacco smoke. Many commonly used products too, such as cosmetics, deodorants, air fresheners, detergents and disinfectants, are falsely scented. And even some natural products such as rubber flooring or wood resins can give off an unpleasant or allergic smell.

We can recover or improve our sense of smell by spending as much time as possible outdoors in clean air, breathing deeply and clearing our lungs. But by making our homes smell more pleasant and natural we can also improve our sense of smell and, with it, our sense of taste.

There are many ways of improving or enhancing the atmosphere in your home. Some are preventative and involve removing or reducing unpleasant smells and their source; others involve introducing natural scents into the home. Some smells last longer than others, so you need to ensure adequate ventilation and extractor systems, even possibly air purifiers, to make your home smell naturally sweeter. You can also help to prevent food smells from lingering by being careful about the materials you use in your home. Don't use heavy velvet drapes, fabric-clad walls and tented ceilings, thick carpets and rugs or upholstery in dining or eating areas where they will absorb odours. Similarly, kitchen surfaces should not be absorbent – ceramic tiles or gloss paints are therefore recommended for walls. And take particular care with open-plan areas, especially

where the kitchen is an integral part of the living space.

Improve the smell of your home with natural products: flowers, herbs and essential oils. Avoid artificial fresheners, particularly spray or aerosol products. Not only do they smell unpleasant but also they are user-unfriendly. Many are more polluting than dust and, if packed in aerosol cans, rely on chlorofluorocarbons (cfcs) as a propellant; these are now known to contribute to depletion of the ozone layer.

AROMATHERAPY

Good scents not only improve air quality but also have specific therapeutic qualities. Treating or improving health with essential oils, herbs and flower extracts is an ancient practice; much traditional medicine in ancient Tibet, China, India and the Middle East was based almost entirely on the use of aromatic substances. In recent years, aromatherapy has re-emerged as an increasingly popular way of dealing with ailments. Aromatherapy makes use of essential oils, derived from flowers, plants, trees and resins. Oils can be burned, put in baths, diluted and placed or massaged on the body. Each essence has different properties that act on the body and mind influencing the emotions and physical wellbeing.

Breathing for health
Good breathing encourages health. Far too many people only breathe shallowly through the mouth, instead of using nose, mouth, diaphragm, muscles and lungs to full potential. Many therapies, religions and philosophies, such as yoga, teach the importance of breathing to bring more oxygen into the blood. Posture too is an important aid to proper breathing and should be applied to sitting, working and sleeping, as well as standing and walking.

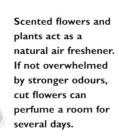
Scented flowers and plants act as a natural air freshener. If not overwhelmed by stronger odours, cut flowers can perfume a room for several days.

ENHANCING YOUR HOME

These pages give advice on simple ways of improving air quality and introducing natural fragrances into the home.

• Air rooms daily by opening windows and doors or using extractor fans, especially in the bathroom and kitchen

• Make your home a non-smoking zone, or set aside one room for smokers that can be aired easily. Alternatively, banish smokers to the garden with an ashtray.

• Remove all synthetic materials from your home: plastics, nylon, vinyl, laminates, medium density fibreboard (MDF) and replace them with natural woods, cottons and other natural materials.

• Use natural materials such as scented beeswax for cleaning and polishing wooden furniture. Beeswax candles also produce a marvellous scent.

• To remove cooking smells, boil pieces of orange, lemon or lime peel, cinnamon sticks or cloves in a small saucepan of water. Keep the kitchen well ventilated and close doors while cooking cauliflower or other strong-smelling vegetables. A piece of stale bread in the cooking water or steamer will help to absorb smells.

• Burn scented candles, joss sticks, smudge sticks, incense or scented oils in pottery burners. Use scented lamp oil. Sprinkle a few drops of oil onto a light bulb or vaporizer ring to permeate the air with a mood-enhancing fragrance.

• Add drops of scented oil to humidifiers or bowls of fresh, tepid water to freshen the air and keep it humid. Change the water daily. Float scented candles in bowls of water, especially when family or friends gather.

• Hang sweet-smelling flowers or bunches of herbs in the kitchen or dining room. Bay leaves, rosemary, sage, lavender and bergamot smell particularly wonderful. Hang dried herbs in cupboards or use them to make pot-pourri or herb pillows.

• Place fresh flowers throughout the home – an inexpensive way of introducing natural scents. Pot bulbs such as hyacinths or lilies in autumn; as their flowers open in spring, their scent will fill the rooms. Make posies from bay, sage, rosemary, lavender, orange blossom and mimosa for bedrooms and bathrooms. Also use freesias, arguably the sweetest-smelling flowers of all.

• Fill dishes with pot pourri and with a few dried culinary herbs, whole cloves and cinnamon sticks or bark.

• Store clothes in cedar-lined chests and drawers, leaving doors and drawers slightly open. Use little lavender or herb bags, cakes of naturally scented soaps or pomanders to keep drawers, and your clothes, sweet smelling. Discourage moths by hanging bunches of fresh or dried bay or rosemary leaves in cupboards, and strips of dried orange peel, allspice berries or cedar chips in drawers.

MAKING A POMANDER
Use an orange, lemon, grapefruit or other citrus fruit. Prick the skin all over with a sharp needle and stud the skin with cloves. Place the fruit in a bag of powdered cinnamon and orris root and shake until well coated. Store in a loosely wrapped acid-free tissue paper for about two weeks, attach ribbon and hang in a wardrobe.

MAKING YOUR OWN POT POURRI
Pot pourri is made from sweet-smelling dried flower petals, aromatic herbs, seeds and spices. You can also add wood shavings, pine cones, cinnamon sticks and other 'woody' textures. A fixative is necessary to preserve the fragrance and you can add extra essential oils but take care not to overdo them, otherwise there will be too many conflicting smells.

Gather flower petals on dry, windless days. Include some buds and small bright flowers for colour. Spread the mixture on paper and dry it in a shaded, airy room. Traditionally, strong-smelling rose petals are used but almost any sweet-scented flowers and herbs can be dried: violets, jasmine, lily of the valley, marigolds, larkspur, pinks, sage, rosemary, bergamot, lavender, lemon verbena and chamomile, even the grey-leaved curry plant.

Once flowers are dry, mix them in a bowl and add a fixative of orris root or gum benzoin. If you wish, add crushed or ground spices – cinnamon, coriander, nutmeg, cloves, allspice, mace, or anise – or leave them whole for a more robust texture. Use 1 tablespoon of fixative to 1.2 litres (5 cups) of petals. Mix together and leave in shallow bowls to scent the air.

To make a moist pot pourri do not dry the flower petals. Instead, spread a layer of petals (usually rose) 10cm (4in) deep in an earthenware crock. Cover with a thin layer of common salt, add another layer of petals, then salt, and so on until the jar is full. Cover and leave in a dark, airy place for 10–14 days. Stir the mixture with a wooden spoon, add dried orange peel, crushed cloves and orris root. Blend and leave sealed and covered for about five to six weeks. Add a few drops of essential oil, reseal for a further two weeks, then decant into small china or pottery jars.

HERB BAGS AND PILLOWS
Herb pillows, filled with peppermint, spearmint and eau-de-cologne mint or bergamot promote healthy sleep, calm the nerves and can soothe away headaches caused by the stresses of a hectic day.

Hop pillows are also good for insomniacs or those who suffer from asthma – you can sprinkle the hop cones with a little vodka before putting them in the bag.

To make your own pillow or bag, use closely woven muslin or cheesecloth. Cut it to the required size and shape and sew around three sides. Stuff the bag full with crumbled or dried herbs – not powdered – and sew up the fourth side. For sleep pillows, add a few drops of rose or lavender oil to stop the herbs crackling. Make an outer covering from silk, cotton or linen. Trim and decorate to taste.

Add a few drops of pine, lavender, rosemary or sage oil with a handful of sea salt to a bath for a relaxing end to a busy day.

ESSENTIAL INGREDIENTS

The ceiling of this bedroom is a feature of its architecture – painting it red further enhances the sense of passion in the room.

FOR RELAXATION and intimacy, create a sensuous bedroom. It can be a pleasure to share with a partner or to enjoy on your own.

Choose relaxing colours. Blue is calming, green refreshing, but both are cool so add warmer neutrals such as creams, beiges, taupes, possibly 'spiced up' with cinnamon. For a minimalist look, consider cool greys, with light-reflecting textures.

Introduce a little red as a symbol of passion – use heart-shaped cushions, or thread red ribbon through the trimming on a duvet cover, or pillow cases. Use rich red mounts for a group of prints or introduce red lamp bases.

If red is too strong, consider pink. Use it for walls and ceiling, or for bedhead wall or carpet only. Lilac is a romantic colour and can create a sophisticated scheme. Combined with subtle greys, deeper mauves, pinks and white, lilac is mysterious and elegant.

Peach and terracotta tones will create a warm and intimate ambience. Use paler versions for main surfaces – pale peach ceiling, deeper tones on walls, and a terracotta carpet – combine with refreshing cream and green contrasts.

All too often ceilings are painted 'safe' white, yet bedroom and bathroom ceilings are the most noticed ceilings in the home. For a really decorative effect use a cloudscape, or carry wallpaper up over the ceiling.

If your bedroom is fairly small, choose curtain colours to blend with the wall and relate the colour or pattern of the bedding to the flooring. Keep patterns fluid and

softly defined; curved shapes are a good choice – avoid bold geometrics. Keep patterned fabrics for windows, drapes and bedding.

Tactile textures are a must and can include strokeable surfaces such as satin, velvet, silk and fur fabrics. Team with muslins and voiles for bed drapes and light-diffusing curtains. Soften flooring with exotic rugs, especially by the bed.

Avoid angular furniture – rounded or chamfered corners are much more pleasing and choose a curvy shape for bed frame or head- and footboards. If you have a rectangular divan, hang bed drapes

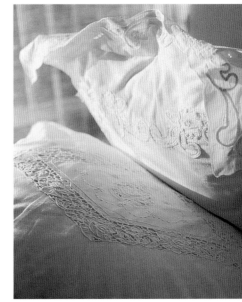

Fresh flowers,
especially if deliciously
scented, will stimulate
the senses. Flowers
also make a good
subject for bedroom
pictures.

from a central coronet above the head end, with flowing fabric to each side, held in position with decorative curtain bosses. A serpentine-backed chaise longue will introduce an attractive form but if space is limited, use a softly rounded chair with a circular lamp and table.

The use of mirrors in bedrooms should be carefully considered. The mirrored ceiling is out. Mirrored wardrobe doors maximize light and space but should not reflect the bed or too much of the room. For good feng shui, wardrobe mirrors should be covered at night and use circular, oval or heart-shaped mirrors.

Lighting should be soft and romantic, even in the daytime. Use delicate light-filtering sheers, muslin or lace drapes or, for a modern look, slatted blinds. Plan after-dark lighting carefully; install several circuits so you can dim task lighting, and enclose pendant light

bulbs in a suitable shade. Soft glow uplighters or wallwashers give off a gentle light.

For an aura of mystery, conceal a floor-mounted uplighter behind a large 'sculptural' plant, in amongst flowers or a group of plants, or behind a screen. This will create attractive shadows. Kinetic lighting is the most magical – glowing candles give a soft, flattering light. Nothing is more wonderful than the flicker of firelight, so if you have a chimney in the room consider installing an open fire.

Bedrooms should also smell enticing – though you should avoid a heavy scent! The smell of fresh air and newly washed linen may be all that is needed or a posy of sweet-smelling flowers. You can create stronger scents by burning scented oils or joss sticks.

Choose pictures for the bedroom with care. Avoid abstracts or disturbing scenes in favour of floral prints or landscape paintings. Feng shui advises against pictures of solitary people or stark settings.

Adding textiles to a bedroom that you automatically want to run your hand across – such as these embroidered lace cushions – introduces the sensuousness of touch to the room (far left).

Softly draped fabrics help to diffuse light in the bedroom, while neutral creams create a relaxed mood (left).

THINGS

A really healthy home needs living things in the form of plants, flowers and possibly animals. Plants encourage physical and emotional wellbeing; carefully chosen and nurtured, they provide a refreshing environment in which you can relax and enjoy a link with the natural world. Indoors, healthy plants, whether bought-in house plants or plants you have grown yourself, can be incorporated into your environment to create a mini ecosystem, which supplies oxygen and helps to control humidity. An outdoor green space, even if it is only a modest patio, provides somewhere to sit calmly away from everyday worries and contemplate nature.

An ideal way of creating a peaceful green space might be a be a plant-filled conservatory or sun room, leading onto a sheltered patio, which provides visual links to a garden beyond. The garden itself can be designed to create a group of outdoor 'rooms', complete with arbours, gazebos, summer houses and water features. You can build a simple bower, with fragrant climbing shrubs sheltering a ' seat, which can be 'upholstered' with herbs such as chamomile or thyme, and surrounded by scented flowers and herbs. Such a scented corner would be much appreciated by the partially sighted and elderly, but can provide a place of peaceful solitude for anyone.

In you live in an apartment, flat or house with only a tiny back yard or front garden, you can still bring colour, greenery and nature into your home.

Put plants in pots outside your front and back doors, window boxes on outside sills, herbs and potted plants on indoor window sills, shrubs, plants and flowers on balconies or plant up hanging baskets. If you have a particularly sunny window sill, you can 'stretch' glazed shelves across the reveal and use them to grow a selection of plants, herbs and flowers that will trail attractively down and climb upwards.

Even if your apartment lacks window sills or balconies, and is situated up several flights of stairs, you can still place shrubs such as bay trees, or palms, outside the entrance to your flat, or plant up a large glass carboy to create a tiny garden in a bottle.

Virtually every room in your home will benefit from house plants: water-loving plants in the bathroom, herbs and other scented plants in the kitchen, romantically soft-coloured and scented plants in the bedroom, and dramatically shaped plants for empty corners, or where you want to create the illusion of greater height. And you can combine plants with candles, lamps, light and mirrors to enhance their presence and increase the effect of wellbeing.

Animals too can play an important part in creating a healthy home. Pets, particularly cats and dogs, are known to have a therapeutic role in combating stress. Snakes, iguanas and other reptiles can bring fascination and beauty into the home and, if such animals do not appeal, an aquarium full of fish is both colourful and therapeutic.

USING HOUSE PLANTS

IF YOUR HOME has no garden, conservatory or greenhouse, and you haven't the time to grow your own plants, then house plants are a most effective way of bringing greenery and nature into the home. There is a huge range of house plants available today from modest African violets through to highly exotic species, many obtainable from garden centres, supermarkets and even your local market stall. As their name suggests, house plants are grown for use indoors; if properly cared for they can survive for many years.

House plants can be chosen purely for their beauty and to add decorative visual elements to the home, but they also encourage health and reduce toxicity. During the daytime, through the process of photosynthesis, plants absorb harmful carbon dioxide and other impurities from the atmosphere and release health-giving oxygen. They also take in water from soil or compost and let it out through their leaves, so assisting humidity levels in the home. To maximize this effect, it is a good idea to group plants rather than place them singly.

PLACING Healthy plants reflect a healthy environment. Although house plants are sold for indoor use, the home is not a natural environment for plants, so you need to create exactly the right conditions for them to thrive. Some plants such as cacti need dry conditions; others such as African violets thrive in a moist atmosphere and are ideal for bathrooms. A few, such as ivy, tolerate shade. Their needs will therefore influence which plants you choose for the various rooms in your home.

In a way, plants are also living accessories that you incorporate into the overall design of your home. You can group them for maximum impact, or stand them singly to fill a gap or to make a design statement. Size, form, colour and texture are therefore important and need to be considered in relation to the space available and the decor of your rooms. Tall, sculptural plants will look good in a large space; smaller, more compact plants will sit happily on a window sill; trailing plants can be used to soften sharp corners, and look particularly effective on shelving. Frondy plants can be trained to grow up walls in your home, supported on sticks or trellis.

Wherever you decide to site your plants, check that light and temperature levels are adequate for their needs. If light is limited, you may want to use special daylight bulbs to encourage growth. Be flexible in your planning, and move

Plants and health

It has been known for some time that house plants are good for your health. They freshen the atmosphere, filter dust and other particles from the environment and some actually absorb pollutants such as tobacco smoke, solvent fumes and formaldehyde. Various plants too such as peace lilies, and philodendron can even counteract the effects of electromagnetic radiation emitted by computers, televisions and microwaves. So impressive are their effects that the American space agency, NASA, which has done considerable research into their anti-polluting qualities, has used plants on board manned space vehicles and space stations to purify and refresh the air.

Anti-polluting plants:

potted chrysanthemums

spider plant (chlotophytum variegatum)

aspidistra lurida

mother-in-law's tongue (sansevieria laurentii)

gerbera daisies

devil's ivy (scindapsus aureus)

variegated ivies (hedera helix & hedera canariensis)

sweetheart plant (philodendron scandens) [anti-radiation]

peace lilies (spathyphyllum wallissi) [anti-radiation]

Whatever the environment in your room – shady, full sun, very dry or high humidity – there is a houseplant that can thrive in it.

plants around sometimes to give them a little 'holiday' and change of scene – they will benefit from this just as much as you do! Your plants may also need feeding with special liquid fertilizer, and dead-heading – removing dead flowers or leaves. Light and water are essential for growth, but check that you do not overwater your plants – a very common fault. Research their needs, and follow cultivation instructions. Some plants such as cyclamens or poinsettias prefer near-dry soil; others need daily watering. It is best to stand pots in water and let plants absorb what they need through their roots but never leave them standing in too much water. In nature, plants are watered from above, which washes their leaves; you may therefore need to spray house plants from time to time.

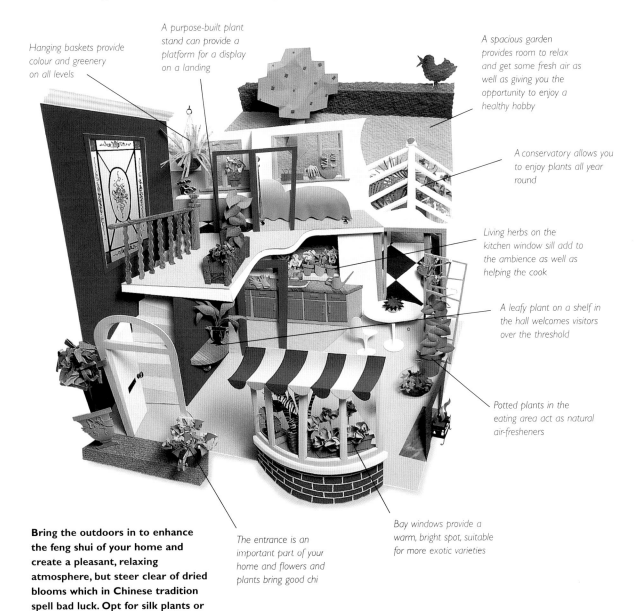

Hanging baskets provide colour and greenery on all levels

A purpose-built plant stand can provide a platform for a display on a landing

A spacious garden provides room to relax and get some fresh air as well as giving you the opportunity to enjoy a healthy hobby

A conservatory allows you to enjoy plants all year round

Living herbs on the kitchen window sill add to the ambience as well as helping the cook

A leafy plant on a shelf in the hall welcomes visitors over the threshold

Potted plants in the eating area act as natural air-fresheners

Bay windows provide a warm, bright spot, suitable for more exotic varieties

The entrance is an important part of your home and flowers and plants bring good chi

Bring the outdoors in to enhance the feng shui of your home and create a pleasant, relaxing atmosphere, but steer clear of dried blooms which in Chinese tradition spell bad luck. Opt for silk plants or flowers if fresh flowers and plants are out of the question.

BRINGING THE OUTSIDE IN

ONE OF THE FINEST ways to relax, reduce tension and de-stress yourself is to work with flowers and green plants, whether or not you have 'green fingers'. Handling earth, compost, seedlings, which you may have grown from the original seed or pip, pricking out, potting on, taking cuttings, pruning and then enjoying the fruits of your labours is very therapeutic. If you have time and space, growing your own plants for indoor use is enormously satisfying. And if you have a garden, conservatory, sun room or greenhouse, there are endless design possibilities.

Another advantage of growing your own plants, or propagating them from existing plants, is that they will tolerate your home environment more easily than bought-in plants. You can also give cuttings away to friends and family, who will return the compliment.

Plants bring health into the home but can also be combined with accessories and furniture to help create a specific design style – an aspidistra in a decorative cache pot placed on a wooden or cast-iron aspidistra stand, surrounded by ferns creates a Victorian feel; neatly shaped bonsai trees, set in shallow containers are oriental in flavour; cacti and succulents mulched with sand or fine gravel look eclectic; beautifully arranged cut flowers, or containers filled with flowering bulbs or corms, such as lilies, hyacinths, freesias or cyclamen, evoke an English country house; while posies of wild flowers and herbs suggest a simple country cottage style.

However, you do need to create the right conditions to enable plants to grow and flourish; they need light, humidity, the right type of soil or compost, and occasional feeding, as well as water. If you have a conservatory, purpose-built porch or sun room, even an atrium created by glazed walls or a roof of 'lantern' light, it should not be too difficult to provide the right conditions and produce a healthy selection of indoor plants, providing a visual link to the outside. You can also grow more unusual items such as citrus trees, indoor vines and exotic vegetables.

Improvise if your home does not include a greenhouse or conservatory. For instance, if you have a particularly sunny window, you can build a simple mini-greenhouse out of wood and glass and attach it to the outside frame. Place shelves inside the structure to hold

There is a great deal of satisfaction to be gained from growing your own flowers and then bringing them into the home to brighten a room.

If you don't have a garden, you can still grow plants on a window sill. A scented herb garden will provide pleasure and a useful product.

Hanging plants fill unused space with vibrant colour and life. Do, however, make sure that containers are watertight.

plants and seedlings, which will grow just as well as in a full-size greenhouse. Remember, however, plants will need some screening from sun and frost. You could build a similar structure on a small outside balcony, or inside a bay window; alternatively, you could glass in a small balcony to create a mini-greenhouse or sun room.

Use any sunny window sill in your home to display or grow herbs and plants, some trailing down, others growing upwards. You can place glass shelves across the window, and mount pots on these, bearing in mind the need to protect them from scorching in direct sunlight. A stained glass panel behind the pots can look very dramatic, and the effect combined with concealed lighting will create even more impact. This can also be a successful way of screening an overlooked window, or of bringing some greenery into a poorly lit basement. In this case, you will need plants such as ivy or ferns, which do not need too much light.

If light allows, the kitchen is a wonderful place to grow herbs such as chives, parsley, sweet basil, and scented-leaved geraniums. Pansies, violas, pot marigolds and nasturtiums will also look good.

You could combine any of these plants with miniature tomato plants – there are some tumbling varieties which look particularly decorative – or small chilli or pepper plants. All these plants will add to the decorative quality of the meal you serve: a green salad garnished with chive flowers and violas; a dish of char-grilled vegetables with oregano marigold and nasturtium flowers; a summer pudding trimmed with appropriate soft fruits, pansy flowers and apple mint will all look wonderfully appetizing.

You can use hanging baskets and window boxes inside the home. Fill baskets with trailing indoor plants and hang them on hooks, or position window boxes on brackets, planting them with trailing plants or flowers. Line window boxes carefully and support them on a drip tray to avoid staining walls and take them down when watering or feeding plants. Alternatively plant in separate pots and use the window box or a jardiniere to hide pots from view. Fill the box with pebbles to increase humidity but prevent the roots from becoming drenched.

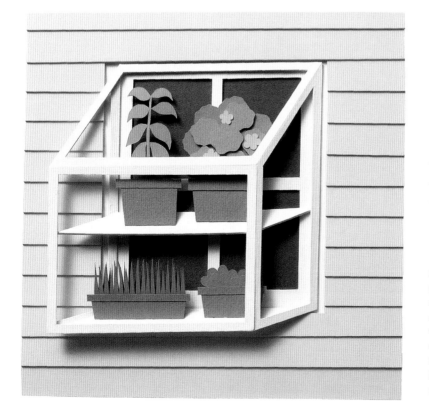

If you don't have the room for a greenhouse or conservatory, try constructing a mini-version at a sunny window. You will then be able to create the kind of habitat that many plants prefer.

RECYCLING CONTAINERS

You can grow plants in almost anything, including old milk churns and preserving pans.

PLANT CONTAINERS lend themselves to recycling and, depending on what they are, can be used both in- and out-of-doors. I devised a very successful indoor herb and plant arrangement for a kitchen, using a recycled 7-tiered saucepan stand, which held plants in differently sized pots. The feet of the stand stood in a deep circular tray and I watered the plants from the top so that the water flowed down through the pots and was collected in the tray. The effect was stylish, filled an empty corner, was virtually trouble free and enabled me to recycle an old possession.

Be creative with containers. A small strawberry or parsley pot with little 'pockets' looks very effective filled with different herbs such as thyme, oregano, chervil, tarragon, lemon verbena or purple basil, topped with a tumbling miniature tomato. The old-fashioned jug-and-basin set from a washstand can be used for an unusual spring indoor garden with various green plants trailing down round the edge and the centre filled with pots of spring bulbs – crocus, hyacinths, narcissus and daffodils. I keep the arrangement fairly low by using short miniature rockery bulbs; the jug is filled with water and cut evergreens to add height, and placed beside the bowl on an old washstand.

Old jugs, teapots, basins, bread crocks, vegetable dishes can all be used as decorative containers, as can metal churns, enamel jugs, old preserving pans and saucepans, if they look decorative. If you are going to place plant and compost directly into these containers, they will need adequate drainage. Drill holes in the bottom of the container and then fill the base with broken crocks (old pieces of terracotta flower pots) and perhaps a few lumps of charcoal to keep the soil sweet.

Old china or earthenware sinks, or wash handbasins, without pedestals, make very successful recycled containers. They are extremely heavy to transport but have the advantage of built-in drainage. Even so they still need filling with broken crocks and gravel for good drainage, and will need to be supported on solid timber or bricks. Mostly used as outdoor displays, they can be very effective in a conservatory, large hallway or dining room.

Redundant fish tanks or an aquarium can be filled with coloured gravel or sand and used to grow a selection of cacti. A round goldfish bowl can be similarly adapted, but might be best with one plant only. Other widemouthed glass jars, with interesting

Recycle imaginatively. Bright yellow tagetes look quite striking growing out of an old pair of boots.

shapes and unusual colours can be similarly planted up, as can the traditional carboy. Different shaped bottles, grouped together and filled with plants, can look stunning, especially if lit with accent lighting at night.

Bird cages too make decorative plant containers, whether circular Chinese style, delicate Victorian metal varieties or modern bamboo and cane. All can be filled with trailing house plants or feathery ferns, hung by the side of a window or from a conservatory roof. Many wire containers such as salad shakers can take on a totally new look when filled with plants.

Old tin and hip baths can be used successfully as plant containers on a patio and in the conservatory, as can old horse

drinking troughs. A metal primer and coats of colourful paint will help to protect containers from the elements. You could use green to fade the container into the environment, or make it a feature with rich, or exciting colours. Other

Gardening enables everyone to be creative. Designing your own containers brings enormous satisfaction.

unusual items include old clothes mangles, sewing-machine stands, even recycled farm machinery, all of which can form a distinctive garden grouping that is more original than pieces of statuary.

Reclaimed chimney pots can also look very decorative used as containers – you can stand a second plant pot inside the rim, or balance a half-circle wire basket on top and plant it up with trailing plants. They are now rapidly becoming collectors' items, but keep your eyes open for work being done on roofs, and see if you can buy directly from a builder. Earthenware conduit pipes also make good containers and can be incorporated into water features.

TERRARIUMS Named after the 19th-century botanist Dr. Nathaniel Ward, who invented them, terrariums are effectively tiny enclosed gardens, ideal for indoor use and slow-growing plants. A sealed terrarium will effectively create its own microclimate, cycling and recycling all the plants' needs inside the glass container. Water in the compost is taken up by the plants and released through the leaves. Moisture then condenses onto the glass top and sides, running back into the compost. As a result a terrarium will only need watering about twice a year. Plants do not need feeding as they manufacture all the food they need. For best results, a terrarium should sit in a light, bright position where it receives about 6 or 7 hours light a day, but not in direct sunlight.

A terrarium is a beautiful self-sustaining garden in miniature, ideal for indoors. Place it in a light position, out of direct sun.

HEALTHY PLANTS and freshly cut flowers bring good feng shui into the home. They enhance energy flows, offset stagnation, improve air quality and can be used to cure various problems.

The colour and type of plant or flower reflects the theory of the five elements and will enhance that element as needed. Cut flowers kept in clear water bring invigorating energies into the home but both flowers and water must be kept fresh; stagnant water is poor feng shui, wilting or dying flowers mean bad luck and will have a negative effect on energy. Artificial flowers, particularly those made of natural materials such as silk or paper, are always preferable to wilting plants and can be used as symbolic cures.

Flower containers too have symbolic meaning. Clear glass vases in curved shapes add a tranquil water chi energy; metal containers help to enhance the metal chi energy, which is good for romance, style and finance. Silver or red will increase the effect, but the colour of flowers should be carefully related to their container. Tall streamlined wooden containers are associated with uplifting tree energy; pyramid shapes increase fire energy; and low bowls or troughs, perhaps containing floating flower heads and candles, are associated with family harmony. Cube or square containers are associated with the soil or earth element.

Plants too must be kept absolutely healthy for good feng shui. The overall size and shape of a plant, and the shape of its leaves will help to create different effects. Tall plants will generate more tree chi energy and if they have pointed or star-shaped leaves will help to move chi energy more quickly; they should not, however, be used in small rooms. Round-leafed plants calm energy flow and can be used to soften dangerous sharp corners in a house and counteract cutting chi. Low bushy plants help to slow down fast-moving chi energy, so are ideal placed in long, narrow halls and corridors or near doors; trailing plants are, like waterfalls, associated with water energy.

It is best to group plants together, using a variety of different shapes and types; their different qualities will complement and balance each other, and provide a better flow of chi energy. Some plants are not suitable for all positions. Plants with thorns or spiky leaves such as yuccas, cacti or palms give off a spiky energy; they should not be positioned too close to a seating area or bed. However, their energy can provide a security device so they are best placed

Red flowers boost fire energy, linked to passion and good luck.

White flowers boost metal energy; tall stems carry wood energy.

in enclosed porches or on window sills to ward off any threat.

In areas which lack natural light such as internal bathrooms, rooms overshadowed by trees or buildings, or a below pavement basement, plants can help to increase chi energy, freshen air and increase humidity. It is difficult to find plants that will thrive in dark conditions, so use special daylight bulbs to encourage growth, stand plants on a sheet of mirror glass or place a mirror behind them to increase any natural daylight. For these conditions, choose plants like ivy (*Hedera helix*) and ferns, which will tolerate shady conditions. As they are associated with water in feng shui, they are particularly appropriate in a bathroom.

Plants can also be used to help improve the problem of low, or sloping ceilings; tall plants, such as palms, aspidistras, or fig trees (*Fiscus*), placed in strategic positions, will help to keep energy flowing upwards and away from the area below the slope, and palms are ideal in the corners. If you combine these with uplighters, hidden amongst the base of the plants, this will throw light up onto the ceiling, also helping to improve the upward flow.

Plants can be used to soften protruding corners, or the sharp corners on furniture and shelves. You can trail a bushy plant down or up to cover the corner and control cutting chi. For this cure, choose a plant with rounded leaves like the philodendron, tradescantia or fiscus. And if you have awkward internal corners, plants with long, sharp pointed leaves, such as palms, spider plants (*Chlorophytum*), yucca or dracaena (*Dracaena marginata*), will prevent stagnation, and get the chi energy circulating.

If you have long corridors, or narrow dark halls, stagger plants on either side, to slow down the fast-moving chi. This cure also works well with plants in pots placed down a narrow path outside the front door. Plants in a porch, or either side of the front door create a feeling of welcome and wellbeing, and can be enjoyed as you go out and come home.

Because house plants help to counteract the effects of electrical radiation from domestic appliances, feng shui suggests putting healthy indoor plants between the source of radiation and where you want to relax, or in the centre of the house. A peace lily (*spathyphyllum wallissi*) is particularly effective.

Other plants can be used in the kitchen and will add natural living energy to the food preparation and storage areas. Tall plants will add tree chi energy, which is harmonious with water and fire. In the bathroom, tall plants help to drain excess water energy.

Yellowish, squat flowers such as marigolds boost earth energy.

Blue ground-covering plants such as aubretia enhance water energy.

CONSERVATORIES AND GREENHOUSES

IF YOU ARE LUCKY enough to have the space – and the budget – a conservatory or sun room can be the most wonderful extension to a healthy home. It can give you extra living space as it may well be used in summer for a dining or sitting room, provide a place for indoor gardening and give you a green centre with a calm, soothing and refreshing ambience where you can reduce tension and restore shattered nerves.

In the 18th and 19th centuries, conservatories were used as camellia houses or orangeries or to plant up unusual plants brought back by intrepid botanists from trips overseas. Today you can use your conservatory to grow exotic plants, indoor vines, unusual fruit and vegetables, and possibly introduce a soothing water feature.

Followers of feng shui will need to call in a consultant before embarking on a conservatory project, because adding a structure to your home will affect energy flows and the natural balance of the environment. But even those who do not practice feng shui may choose to call in experts, who will advise on ventilation, watering and screening systems as well as choice of plants. They will also be able to advise on lighting and heating systems, many of which are now self-adjusting.

A conservatory or sun room can range from a large bought-in structure, which includes everything from furniture, fittings and plants, through to a small self-built lean-to greenhouse, which can be fixed against an outside wall, and which will provide a small, sheltered green space where you can potter with your plants. You can even create a very successful mini-conservatory by glassing in a porch or flat roof.

PLANTING The plants you choose depend on the type of conservatory you want to create. For a 'Return to the Raj' type, which was popular in the Victorian and Edwardian eras, you could furnish with cane, wicker and a ceiling fan and plant according to the period: parlour palms, aspidistras, ferns and other plants popular at the time.

Alternatively a conservatory can be planted for all-year colour, with flowering plants, shrubs, bulbs and so on planned to come into bloom at different seasons. Foliage plants will also be important; choose them for colour – green, deep red or bronze; variegated – for their texture and for the colour of their flowers. For all-year interest, remember to include some evergreen plants.

Grouping and tactile impact are also important, so aim to use different textured leaves; group tall, tree-like shrubs, trailing feathery ferns, spreading glossy-leafed varieties, low compact shapes, with spiky ones. You might also want to experiment with citrus fruit, which look wonderful in pots and will reward you with your own lemons, kumquats or limes. If you are patient you can grow these from pips.

A greenhouse or conservatory enables you to enjoy plants all-year round. Group them by height and colour for interest.

Warmth and luxurious green plants refresh the spirit and calm the nerves. A lean-to greenhouse (below) provides space for growing plants but, if insulated, also traps heat.

Light and healthy green plants encourage good feng shui and are soothing and refreshing. Adding a conservatory (above and right) changes the home's energy balance so it is best to check positioning with a consultant.

SOLAR GREENHOUSES

Solar systems can also be used to bring on seedlings, grow plants and herbs – even food. A solar greenhouse, which is attached to the house on the sun-facing side is a different concept from a conservatory or sun room, although it can be used similarly for leisure purposes and as an extra room. With adequate thermal insulation the warmth can be 'trapped' and used to heat the area in the evening, and to warm water for the plants.

It is also possible to use solar energy to heat a separate greenhouse, warm propagators and so on. Interestingly, this is a development of the 18th century orangery (and later the Victorian glasshouse), which was a separate building from the rest of the house but it had a thick-brick back wall, usually on the north side, with a system of chimneys and open fires on the outside, which heated the brick; the rest of the sun-facing walls were glazed. In winter, maximum use was made of the sun to keep the temperature suitable for growing citrus fruit, pineapples, vines and so on but extra heat was provided by lighting the fires and letting out the warmth slowly. This is another reason why walled gardens were so popular, and still are – the warmth of the sun retained in the brick on a walled kitchen garden provided ideal growing and ripening facilities for fruit such as peaches and apricots to be eaten in the house.

GARDENS

A formal herb garden, featuring the beautiful contrast of purple and green sage, complements this Gothic summerhouse with trailing wisteria vines.

Box hedge is a traditional border for English gardens and will provide background greenery all year round.

EVEN THE SMALLEST back yard or tiny town garden can become a beautiful outdoor greenspace. Don't discount your front garden either, or the narrow strip running along the side of the house; these areas can also be designed and planted up very effectively.

Before beginning, you need to consider which way your garden faces and the amount of natural light it receives. Soil type too is an important consideration. If you have a north- or north-east-facing garden, which is shady for most of the day, look for shade-loving plants or those which thrive in damp conditions. If you have a sunny south- or south-west-facing garden with lots of good drainage, and a tendency to dry out when the sun shines, you may find it better to concentrate on creating a Mediterranean-style garden, full of aromatic and tactile herbs and plants that thrive on dry conditions and attract wildlife such as birds, bees and butterflies.

If you want a frankly sensual garden, choose plants for their scent, touch and visual quality and plan paths to meander amongst them, so you brush against them as you stroll by. You could plant small cushion-like herbs such as thyme, chamomile and feverfew between paving stones on a patio or garden path, so the scent is released when you walk on them. Fragrant plants in pots close to a front or back door or window can be enjoyed every time you pass by and can also be placed close to any sitting-out or eating area. If you want to give the patio, terrace or

veranda a Tuscan or French Riviera flavour, add trellising and grow climbing plants up over it, forming a canopy over the top as a natural screen – a vine would be even more appropriate.

If your garden is fairly small, you could consider paving most of it, perhaps with one or two raised beds, and use plants in containers to provide greenery, colour and fragrance. One of the advantages of this type of garden is that you can change the planting to suit the season, perhaps filling the edge of pots with spring, summer or autumn flowers, planting a more permanent fixture, such as a flowering shrub, in the centre. You can also move containers around fairly easily, so any plants which need a little more sun or light can be moved to a better position for a few weeks, giving another group of plants a refreshing holiday in the shade. For good effect, vary the height of plants and containers.

Colour is important. Plan for background greenery all year round – this can be provided by evergreens – and use small trees and shrubs that look good in winter, even without foliage. Eucalyptus has wonderful silver-grey stems and foliage; the stems of cornus, or dogwood, turn deep red or golden orange in autumn lasting right through the winter; the bark of a silver birch tree is one of the most magical sights against a clear blue winter sky. Then use coloured flowers, plants and flowering shrubs to create mood or uplift you. Red, yellow, orange, purples and strong pinks are dynamic and energizing;

Varying shades of green and soft, muted mauve set against natural paving stone encourage a feeling of calm and restfulness.

Colour in the garden creates mood and atmosphere just as it does indoors. Reds, yellows and purple are active, energizing colours that provoke a sense of excitement.

green, blue and white are more calming and low-key. Don't worry about colours clashing, they never do in nature.

If you prefer to be a little more restrained, you could colour-grade your plants in beds, borders or a group of containers. Use yellow and white with rich green and greyed foliage; mix yellow and orange with warm copper-coloured leaf plants such as berberis, cornus, or copper beech; show off deep blues and purples against paler mauves and pinks, with subtle greyed and silver foliage.

If you are lucky enough to have plenty of space you might be able to design the whole garden as a series of outdoor rooms: a green room, enclosed by shrubs or neatly clipped hedges as a place to sit and relax; a herb garden, possibly planned in the style of a traditional 16th-century knot garden; a water garden complete with pool and bridge over the stream; a childrens' play area with tree house, climbing frame, swing and sandpit; an outdoor dining area, complete with table, chairs and barbecue – the possibilities are endless.

Try also to grow some of your own food. Use a walled area if you have the space, or in a series of raised beds. If space is limited, you can pop unusual vegetables and fruit among the flowers and plants; many are designed to be grown in pots or hanging baskets so they can be included in even the smallest patio. Soft fruit, peaches, apricots, plums, apples and pears can be trained fan or espalier fashion against trellising, forming a screen

or natural division between areas, and you will enjoy the fresh fruit at harvest time – there is nothing more wonderful than a fresh peach, fig or mulberry picked and eaten warm, straight from the tree.

Aim to garden organically, especially if you plan to grow your own fruit and vegetables. Organically grown food is much healthier but also tastes more delicious. Organic gardening will also encourage more wildlife into the garden, with no danger of them being poisoned.

The important thing is to cultivate food in nature's own way in organic soil, which is full of natural minerals and fed organically as well. One of the most successful, and inexpensive, ways of doing this is to use compost to mulch and

feed the plants. You can make compost either in a traditional compost heap hidden away in a corner or in special composting drums and bins. In a small garden, an enclosed container or a heap covered with black impermeable sheeting is more socially acceptable!

Pest control too should be organic. Don't use sprays or insecticides. Instead encourage wildlife to rid your plants of pests such as black, green and white flies. You can even buy some natural predators such as lacewings, or soil-aerating worms.

To start you off on your organic garden, buy plants, seeds and products from recommended organic suppliers – there are many available today and they can provide useful advice.

Making compost

Most leftover foods – old vegetable trimmings, tea leaves, coffee grounds, fruit cores and rinds – can be composted into a nourishing fertilizer for the garden. You can also include small scraps of paper, cotton waste, grass clippings and autumn leaves.

Use a special container, either home-made or purchased from a garden supplier. These range from metal or wood containers to special 'tumbling' containers for small gardens. Site compost in a handy shaded position, away from playing or dining areas and screen from view with trellising, fencing or plants. Line the container with newspaper, and collect your kitchen waste in a sheet of newspaper or old paper bag, which can be added to the compost bin. There are several natural ways of activating the breakdown of waste including using liquid from the comfrey plant, which you can grow for the purpose, or seaweed. Special 'wormeries' are available from garden specialists; the worms live on the refuse and speed up the composting process.

Widespread and long-term use of pesticides may be linked to serious disorders such as leukaemia. By gardening organically, you avoid introducing harmful pesticides and other chemicals into the food chain as well as producing healthier, tastier and pollutant-free vegetables.

FENG SHUI GARDENS

A feng shui garden aims to provide a calm setting in which to meditate and philosophize. It should echo nature and be as natural-looking as possible. Rocks, for example, are appreciated for their colour, texture and form. Unlike traditional Western garden practice, they are are not covered with alpine plants, although grasses and other sculptural plants can be incorporated into the design to enhance the effect of the rocks.

Straight lines should be avoided and gentle curved and S-shaped paths should be designed to meander along, as the view and mood changes. In some traditional 'mobile' feng shui gardens, screens, trellising and walls are used to create a series of outdoor rooms, so the visitor moves from one experience to another. Bridges over water should curve gently upwards to encourage you to look into the water and to contemplate the reflections. A willow with branches dipping gracefully into the stream is a powerful water symbol.

No feng shui garden is complete without a water feature. Its surface should be reflective and the shape curvaceous; on a flat site, build an interestingly shaped pond; on a sloping site aim for the more naturalistic look of a gently flowing stream, waterfall or rivulets. Water must be kept moving, so use a pump to recycle the water. The pump must be silent because the sound of running water is an integral part of the overall effect of the feng shui garden.

A garden planned according to the principles of feng shui should contain a water feature to promote the flow of energy.

LOW-ALLERGEN GARDENS

HAY FEVER, asthma, pollen and other allergies are extremely widespread. In the United Kingdom, more than 3 million people suffer from asthma, and one in ten suffers from pollen and other allergies, and the effects counteract the pleasure of ordinary gardens or plant life. However, if you or a member of your family suffers from any of these ailments, you can create a special, low-allergen garden.

If you have the space, select a suitable site, which should be away from the rest of the garden, or create your whole garden as a low-allergen space using walls, fences and trellising as an alternative to hedges and shrubs. Design a water feature which will create an atmosphere of peace and calm amongst the green foliage and plants and keep the air moist.

It is essential to choose the plants carefully. Some evergreen plants and shrubs are low in pollen and are therefore suitable. Flowering plants that are insect-pollinated are more suitable than wind-pollinated flowers because the pollen is heavy and too large to inhale; it is also not blown so widely into the air. Avoid plants with a heavy scent and replace them with sweet-smelling herbs such as mint, rosemary or oregano.

If you personally have hay fever, plan and do structural work in your garden during the winter, and plant the garden in early spring when the pollen count is low. During high summer when the pollen count may be high, enjoy or work in your garden in early morning, or on greyer, cooler days.

Hay fever and other allergies can make outdoor life a misery. By making some simple changes and introducing specialist plants, you can create a low-allergen garden.

Use gravel for mulching

Use paving instead of grass lawns

Avoid rotting vegetation and compost, which release mould spores

Plant low-allergen ground cover to avoid weeds

Replace heavily scented plants with lightly fragrant herbs

Choose insect-pollinated plants

Take out unsuitable plants and replace with low-allergen varieties

Remove hedges and replace with painted fence or wall

This low-allergen garden on display at London's Chelsea Flower Show in 1994 was sponsored by the National Asthma Campaign in the UK.

Low-allergen plants

Choose plants that are insect-pollinated, rather than wind-pollinated.

Most shrubs are insect-pollinated, with the exception of ones that are heavily scented, such as: *honeysuckle, jasmine and philadelphus*.

Most flowers are also insect-pollinated, but those who are pollen sensitive should avoid: *asters, carnations, chrysanthemums, dahlias, daisies, dandelions, goldenrod, pinks and sweet williams*.

Heavily scented plants that can also cause a problem include: *daffodils, freesias, hyacinths, roses and sweet peas*.

Most trees are wind-pollinated and should be kept well away from the house. Particular ones to avoid are: *ash, beech, birch, elder, hazel, horse chestnut, lime, oak, pine, plane, poplar, sycamore, willow and yew*.

Herbs are insect-pollinated, but pick them before they flower to avoid any possible allergens.

PETS

Guardians of the home, dogs bring life, energy and companionship – in feng shui, they are associated with earth energy. For young children, smaller animals, such as rabbits, provide something to cherish.

PETS, especially cats and dogs, are very much an integral part of life in North America, Australia, Great Britain and some areas of Europe and are often treated as one of the family. A well-cared for family pet can help in the emotional development of children, giving them the chance to love and care for something smaller and more helpless than themselves, so increasing their awareness of others' needs. A pet can also give a child a 'safety valve': something to hug, stroke, love, and talk to, which can be very therapeutic. Keeping a pet can also help to teach a child the facts of life as well as preparing them for the natural cycle of life from birth to death.

Children in both town and country have little contact with wild or the larger domesticated animals; they may be fortunate enough to visit nearby city farms or a wildlife park, where, however, animals are not always seen in truly natural conditions. And zoos and circuses often give a completely wrong impression of animals, so that keeping a pet is often a child's main contact with the animal world.

Animals and pets can also be stress busters for adults and teenagers. Many people, especially the elderly, live solitary lives and a cat or dog can be a comforting friend. They welcome you when you return home, and provide a living creature to talk to and fuss over, possibly preventing their owner from becoming depressed. Stroking and grooming a cat, rabbit, guinea pig, gerbil, hamster

or dog is known to be therapeutic; it relieves tension, reduces pulse rate and lowers blood pressure. The work of guide dogs for the blind, partially sighted and deaf also provides an example of how animals can provide practical help for humans.

Dogs in the house also provide security. They offer a shield, without the need to turn the house into a fortress, particularly for those living alone, because burglars are likely to be deterred by a bark or growl. They also offer protection when walking in city or town streets, or along lonely country lanes. The very fact that a dog needs regular exercise and to be taken for walks, encourages their owners to take a healthy walk twice a day, another way of reducing tension and keeping fit.

Walking a dog can also be an antidote to loneliness and a good way of meeting people, particularly if you are new to an area or neighbourhood. If you don't want to keep a dog yourself, you could always offer to walk a dog for someone else.

Long-haired cats or dogs can be problematic for those who suffer from asthma or allergies. Short-haired cats, such as Burmese, Siamese or Abyssinians, can be suitable; they are supremely elegant and can be enjoyed for their feline grace. A more recent breed, which is almost hairless, is the Devon Rex. The sound of a purring cat is extremely soothing and can be a sensuous experience. All short-haired cats are pedigree and must be obtained from breeders rather than pet shops. Some cross-breeds are also short haired and will consequently be fairly low-allergen. Some dogs too, notably poodles, which have fleece-like fur, can also be suitable. Special vacuum cleaners are available with cleaning heads and filters that deal with pet hairs and consequently will help to control breathing problems associated with animal hair.

For those who want animals in the house but do not want cats or dogs, smaller mammals such as mice, gerbils, guinea pigs or rabbits can be pleasing alternatives. Most are usually kept in cages to keep them safe from predators, and for reasons of hygiene. Very small mammals too can disappear down holes in the floor. For their comfort and health, cages must be of a good size, and for rabbits or guinea pigs, a large hutch can be provided for daytime use. This can be put into the garden in good weather and moved about so that the animal has access to fresh grass – also a good way of keeping the grass short. Cages must be kept clean, and children should be encouraged to clean them out on a regular basis; soiled straw, hay and shavings can be recycled in the compost heap.

Most species of small mammals will be fairly content in this situation but birds, which fly free in the wild, will become frustrated if kept in cages, and often stop singing or begin to moult. I would not recommend keeping a caged bird, but, if you have a large garden with space for a proper aviary, birds might be a consideration. Homing pigeons too are favoured by some people, and offer an absorbing pastime. Trained to fly long distances before returning to their pigeon loft, they get plenty of opportunity to exercise their wings.

There are, unfortunately, various down sides to keeping pets, particularly cats and dogs. They require constant attention, which can make holidays difficult, and consume a great deal of food, which is often specially formulated, canned and packaged for them, adding cost and contributing to the problem of household waste. Cans are now recyclable, but foil containers and plastic are not. It is often advisable to train cats and dogs to eat scraps and family leftovers, and to give them fresh fish, meat and offal. It is difficult, but not impossible, to convert carnivores to vegetarianism, although most veterinary experts advise a dog's diet should be one-third meat, including offal, with cereals and vegetables; cats need three-quarters of their diet to be meat and/or fish and poultry.

Some vets also specialize in alternative health therapies for pets avoiding the artificial remedies, using homeopathy, acupuncture, herbs and even aromatherapy.

FISH

Cats, although beautiful and aesthetically pleasing, are highly predatory, and can kill wild birds, mice, shrews, and even squirrels, which can be distressing for their owners. They may also poach fish from a un-netted pond. However, don't scold or punish an animal for bringing in trophies; it is a sign of their natural instincts and regard for their owners.

Within the home, animals can do damage – cats in particular are known to be home wreckers! They will shred upholstery, splinter the legs on furniture, 'revitalize' the carpet into a fuzzy construction when sharpening their claws, shin up drapes and curtains, even chew wool blankets, rugs, flooring and clothes. However, most animals can, and should, be trained to use an alternative outlet such as a scratching board. All cats too should have access to the outside world via a cat flap.

An untrained dog will also have a tendency to soil pavements and parks, which is unhealthy and extremely anti-social. Training to avoid this involves providing a clean litter tray daily so that you can train yourself and your dog to be more hygienic and socially aware. Many parks and open spaces now have designated areas for dog excreta, or specialized containers for dog faeces. Dog owners must consider others and when walking their dog should use a 'pooper scooper' to scoop up faeces, or even bring them home to dispose of down the lavatory.

The harmful Toxocara *canis* found in faeces can survive in soil for over two years, so your dog should not foul on the lawn or borders, especially if there are children in the house. Strict hygiene is essential; never eat while playing with an animal. Always wash your hands thoroughly after grooming, feeding and playing with a pet and teach your children to do the same.

Finally, pets such as cats and dogs should always wear a collar, bearing its name, and your address and telephone number.

Walking a dog is very enjoyable and a cheap, effective way of keeping fit. Allowing a dog to foul public places, however, is anti-social and spreads disease.

AN AQUARIUM filled with colourful fish can be the ultimate design accessory; it can add colour and a constantly moving image to any room in the house. Built into a wall between two rooms, it can create an impression of space, light and life. But fish are not only beautiful, they are also known to create a soothing environment and have a profoundly calming effect. They also need very little upkeep.

Until recently, glass was the only material used for aquariums and fish tanks, but now clear acrylic sheeting is available that is safer because it is more shatter-proof. It can also be moulded so that aquariums come in a wide range of shapes from semi-architectural structures to the more conventional rectangular fish tank.

Aquariums should be sited where they are most safe and easily visible. Nothing should be placed on top of the tank. You should seek professional advice about which types of fish are most suitable, how many, and which can live together. Bat fish, angel fish, puffers, moray eels, boxer crabs, cleaner waffle and tang can live together but others may well be predators that will kill the other occupants. It is important too to avoid overcrowding, which will kill or distress the fish, and to avoid over-feeding.

Aquariums combine water and electricity – to light, pump, aerate and circulate the water – so must be installed by a qualified expert.

An aquarium full of fish brings beauty and calm into the home.

FISH AND FENG SHUI

Fish in outdoor pools and water features or inside in aquariums, tanks or bowls are good feng shui because they are believed to bring luck to their owners. They are also known to be soothing and calming, which is why they are recommended for hospital and dentists' waiting rooms. In the home, they should be positioned in the east or south-east of the centre of your home.

Fish are thought to stimulate chi by their movement, depending on their shape, colour and their behaviour. Fast-moving fish, darting back and forth, create a dynamic flow of chi energy; more slow-moving, rounded fish will calm down chi energy. As in interior design, brightly coloured fish stimulate the flow of energy; more muted coloured fish will create a more relaxing ambience.

For good feng shui, the tank should be 'landscaped' with natural materials such as rocks, shells and pebbles, combined with appropriate living plants. Plastic decorations must be avoided.

Fish are particularly auspicious in feng shui. Their flowing movements activate healthy chi and they are believed to stimulate wealth and abundance. But they must be healthy.

Fish are known to have therapeutic qualities. Their presence can relieve high blood pressure and lower stress levels. They can make a very positive contribution to a healthy home.

ENCOURAGING WILDLIFE

A wildlife garden is ecologically balanced. Plants attract insects and other creatures that remove pests naturally, without pesticides.

ENCOURAGING various species of wild animals into your garden is both life-enhancing and a very natural way of bringing living things into your home. Flowering shrubs, herbs and scented flowers will all encourage bees and insects, and shrubs such as buddleia, appropriately nicknamed the butterfly bush, will attract one of the most beautiful of wild things – the butterfly, from simple lilac blues to the truly magnificent Peacock and Camberwell Beauty. They in turn will pollinate the plants, and bees will make honey from the nectar.

If you have a large enough garden and lots of fruit trees and flowering shrubs and plants, you could consider keeping bees, which is a most rewarding hobby. Site hives well away from the house, and encourage children not to go too close unless accompanied by an adult. They will enjoy helping to harvest the honey and making beeswax candles. My great aunt kept bees in the middle of a cherry orchard, and from a very young age I used to help her; she always insisted that I go and 'talk to the bees' on my arrival at her house,

to keep them in touch with what had been happening in my life, and as a result I was never stung.

Wildlife can also help to keep your garden naturally pest free. Frogs, toads and water insects in a pond will help to keep the water clean, and keep the slug population down; you may also gain the extra benefit of seeing dragonflies hovering over the pond or pool in the summer months.

Hedgehogs are another gardeners' friend, because they prevent slugs and snails from eating great holes in your hostas and other precious plants. You can feed them yourself, but only feed them occasionally or they won't control the slug and snail population. Hedgehogs love soft fruit but do not use netting to protect strawberries or the hedgehog could become enmeshed in it. In autumn, search for slumbering hedgehogs in piles of garden waste before setting fire to it; also check compost heaps.

A healthy garden will also encourage bird life, and their song will be a pleasing addition to your home. If you feed birds, make sure that any bird table, or nuts are placed in such a way that cats cannot reach them. Place a bird table away from walls, fences or convenient window sills and fix something round the base to prevent cats from climbing up and using it as a dining table. Squirrels too are notoriously good at poaching food intended for birds; you can buy feeders which allow birds to eat but are designed to keep other animals at bay.

It is said that if you talk to bees, you won't get stung. Keeping them is a skill but, if successful, they will provide you with fresh honey and beeswax.

Because of its delicate colour and strong scent, lavender is a popular garden plant which is also grown commercially. Butterflies and bees also find the pungent, purple bush irresistible.

CREATING AN ECO

–FRIENDLY HOME

160

A HEALTHIER HOME

170

A RESOURCE-FRIENDLY HOME

A HOME

In the first section of this book you will have seen how good spatial planning, interesting design, and sensitive use of colour and furnishings can all contribute to creating a pleasant ambience and healthy home – where you can live in harmonious surroundings.

But a healthy home is also about safety and environmental friendliness. As home owners, particularly in the West, we consume vast quantities of valuable resources such as water and energy on a relentless day-by-day basis. We also generate mountains of household waste from food to unnecessary packaging. We may also introduce toxic or chemical pollutants into the home in the form of household cleaners, sealants, plastics and foam-filled furniture, which are themselves unhealthy and contribute to the problems of pollution both inside and outside the home.

Few of us can afford to design and build our own homes from scratch nor can we necessarily manage to completely redecorate and refurnish every room in one go. Instead we usually move into a property that will need some initial remedial or cosmetic work before we can turn it into the home we want. It may, for instance, contain some harmful or toxic materials such as lead or asbestos, which are now known to be dangerous.

This section, therefore, looks at some of the toxic substances and other sources of pollution, which may already be present in your home, and suggests ways of dealing with them. It also offers advice on choosing and using safer, more environmentally friendly products in the home, suggestions on what to keep and what to replace of the existing fabric and, if you wish, how to apply the ancient principles of feng shui in order to heal your home, correcting a negative or stagnant interior and improving the flow of energy throughout the home.

The following pages also include many practical ways in which you can become more energy and resource conscious: by using solar or other forms of alternative power, by insulating your home to conserve energy, by introducing simple measures to avoid wasting water, without losing your quality of life, by cutting down on consumption generally and by learning to recycle a whole range of household products.

Most of these suggestions can be introduced and implemented quite simply into your daily life. They will ensure not only that your home is truly healthy and in tune with the environment but also, in some cases, may provide you with very useful and thrifty ways of saving money.

SURVEYING FOR POLLUTANTS

WHEN WE BUY A NEW HOME we usually call in an expert to survey it for us. The survey will warn of structural faults, subsidence, plumbing and electrical defects and the need for damp or infestation control as well as assessing the value. But we rarely request a survey for pollutants present in the fabric or brought into the home by other means.

Most of us today are aware of the problems and hazards of environmental pollution but not everyone is aware that the home itself can be polluting. According to the US Environment Protection Agency, indoor pollution may in some cases be ten times as high as that of the street outside. According to the EPA also, air pollution in the home as well as exposure to polluting consumer products can carry serious health risks even though home owners perceive these as less worrying than, say, pollution from landfill sites. Problems can also be intensified by our tendency to over-insulate and seal our homes, so trapping and circulating unhealthy vapours or gases – one very good reason for remembering to open windows.

Pollutants in the home come in various forms, from invisible radiation through to cigarette smoke and dust mites. Other common health hazards include asbestos, lead, pressed boards bound with urea-formaldehyde resins and plastics. Some such as asbestos, once commonly used as an insulator, or lead pipes and lead-based paint may already be present in your home, remnants of previously acceptable building practices. Other pollutants, particularly various vapours and fumes, may be introduced into the home with the increasing use of chemicals and synthetic materials. Formaldehyde, for instance, is one of the most harmful. Used in literally hundreds of household products and building materials and once commonly used as a cavity-wall insulator, it gives off noxious fumes that can cause skin irritation and breathing difficulties. Fortunately its use is now largely banned. Plastics too, particularly PVCs (polyvinylchlorides), also produce harmful fumes as do a whole range of products from cleaning materials through to glues, adhesives and sealants.

Other sources of pollution include radon, an invisible, tasteless and odourless gas which may be present in the actual structure of the house or seep in from surrounding areas, and other forms of radiation emitted from various household appliances such as computers, televisions and microwaves.

Not all dangers are obvious – fumes do not always smell – and their effects are usually cumulative. Nor is any one home likely to contain every sort of pollutant. But by and large it is possible to take preventative measures to deal with almost all household pollutants. In the case of existing pollutants, it is best to start by taking professional advice. Asbestos, for instance, must be professionally removed as it only becomes truly dangerous when disturbed. Experts too can advise on the presence of radon, and floors and walls can be sealed or covered with radon-impermeable materials. Installing good ventilation systems, especially in basements and on the ground floor, will also help to clean air. You can minimize on pollutants by cutting down on electrical appliances and choosing natural products to clean, decorate and furnish your home.

Surveying for a new home

If you are buying land on which to build or thinking about a newly built house that is part of a development, check the history of the site. It is not wise to buy or build on top of a landfill site, over a salt, tin, coal or other mineral mine, or a granite, stone, marble or clay quarry, nor over an area with many underground streams.

If building your own home, you may also want to have a geomagnetic survey. This looks into gradients in the earth's magnetic field and establishes the presence of any negative substances that might affect the health of the occupants. The survey is carried out in relation to the contours of the site: any distorted trees for instance are regarded as suspicious as they may point to geomagnetic abnormalities and the surrounding area is measured carefully, usually with a proton magnetometer. The survey should also detect potential areas of radioactivity.

A professional surveyor or architect should plot the results of such a survey on a contoured site plan, enabling the house to be built in the most favourable position.

Asbestos, once used as insulator around pipes or boilers or in ceiling tiles, must be removed by experts. Removal disturbs asbestos fibres, which can cause respiratory or other disorders

Plastics of all kinds from furniture through to packaging release harmful fumes

Dust mites can exacerbate asthma

Cigarette smoke is one of the most serious indoor pollutants. Health risks from active or passive smoking include emphysema, lung cancer and heart problems

Petrochemical-based paints, stains or varnishes release harmful fumes

Sulphur dioxide from coal fires

Foam-filled furniture is highly flammable and produces toxic fumes if it combusts

Lead-based paint, once commonly used as a drying agent is highly poisonous; it must be removed carefully

Nitrogen dioxide or carbon monoxide from badly maintained gas cookers, heaters or wheelie heaters

Lead pipes can poison water and must be removed

Pesticides and fungicides used in timber treatments can be toxic

Phthalates from vinyl floor tiles and carpet backing

Radon, an invisible gas, that may be present in construction materials or seep in from outside

Houses, whether old or new, may contain a surprising number of pollutants. You should aim to remove these, with professional help if necessary.

Formaldehyde, a VOC, used in cavity-wall insulation, chipboards, disinfectants, carpets and various building materials, can cause asthma and bronchitis. Very common in newly built homes

Volatile organic compounds (VOCs) in paints, glues, polishes and construction materials can cause eye irritation, headaches and possible nerve damage

REMOVING POLLUTANTS

FOR MAXIMUM HEALTH you need to look carefully at the materials used to build, decorate and furnish your home and change or replace toxic or hazardous substances with natural non-toxic materials.

TIMBER TREATMENTS

You may need professional advice to establish the health of any timber in your home because treatments are not always obvious. Some timbers, particularly those on window and door frames, may have been treated with preservative that contains toxic chemicals or creosote. Beams, joists and roof timbers may have been professionally protected against wood-worm and dry rot with substances that are dangerous. If this is the case, you may want to replace certain timbers; others, such as exterior woodwork, could be carefully stripped and a more user-friendly preservative or stain used. Some stains and paints are 'micro-porous', allowing wood to 'breathe' so it is less likely to suffer from damp and decay and will not need restaining or repainting so often.

If you are having timbers protected against decay or infestation, or are buying new frames, you can insist that user-friendly materials are used. Some can be impregnated with a borax which prevents fungus from developing or insect eggs from hatching. This can be injected into existing timbers as well, including exterior greenhouses, cold frames and sheds and will not harm plant life.

There are also other special non-chemical methods of treating fungal decay. Woodworm and other beetles can be treated with permethrin (a derivative of pyrethrum), or in some cases a special heat treatment, originally developed in Scandinavia, can be used. Always check which materials or chemicals are being used and insist on non-toxic alternatives, even though these are likely to be more expensive and may not carry the same length of guarantee as more conventional treatments.

FLOORINGS

Vinyl floorings often appear, unsuccessfully, to look like natural products. Commonly used in the home, they are wasteful of natural resources and release harmful fumes. There are many healthier alternatives.

Many hard floorings come directly from the earth and are quarried. They include marble, slate, granite, various natural stones, including flagstones, although there are reconstituted stones now available. Even volcanic lava is now being used for floors. Other natural floorings include quarry and ceramic tiles, terracotta *carres*, encaustic tiles and bricks. Many hard floorings will need sealing or treating in some way to make them impervious but avoid PVC varnishes and sealants in favour of more natural alternatives.

Wood too is a natural product which comes in many different forms for flooring, from simple planks, decking or tongue-and-groove floorboards, to intricately inlaid parquet and special 'floating' laminated panels. Most wood needs a non-slip sealant but here too environmentally friendly substances are available. If you are installing a new wood floor, consider using recycled timber.

Some resilient floorings are also made from natural materials. Cork, for example, comes from the bark of the cork oak tree and is then made into tiles. These need sealing so they do not swell and 'push up' if they get wet and they must be laid on a damp-proof subfloor. There are some pre-sealed tiles available, which are best for 'wet' situations. Cork is not only ecologically sound but is also a very good insulator and is warm and comfortable underfoot.

Linoleum, or lino, is obtained from natural materials: linseed oil, resin from pine trees, wood flour from deciduous trees mixed with inorganic fillers, such as chalk, and calendered onto a hessian or jute backing, then cured in special drying ovens, creating a very flexible, hard-wearing and resilient floor. Lino can be bought in sheet form or as tiles.

Rubber is another natural product. Made from the liquid sap of the rubber tree, it is available as tiles and in sheet form, often has an interestingly textured surface, and comes in some stunning colours. It is bouncy and quiet underfoot and needs sealing with a special sealant as it perishes if it becomes too wet.

There are softer options – the so-called natural floorings such as sisal and sea-grass matting, coir and coconut matting, rush matting, jute and hemp. These are mostly available in their natural or neutral colours although they can be dyed, stencilled with a pattern or trimmed with a decorative border. Many of them have a backing for extra stability but make sure that this is a natural rubber backing rather than PVC.

Carpets have long been the underfoot luxury but do choose a natural fibre, either 100 per cent wool or an 80/20 'mix' (80 per cent wool/20 per cent nylon) or cotton. Some more exotic carpets and rugs are made from silk. Some carpets and other soft floor coverings have been treated with chemicals to make them stain and dirt repellent and to bulk up pile.

These treatments are toxic so check floor coverings before buying. It is possible to remove the treatment with cleaning but is better to avoid them all together.

FABRICS AND SOFT FURNISHINGS

Always try to use natural rather than artificial fibres in the home. For upholstery, consider wool, cotton, linen, silks or their various combinations. Union, for example, which is a hard-wearing fabric used for loose covers and some upholstery, is a combination or 'union' of linen and cotton. Some may, however, contain a small quantity of artificial fibres, which will make them crease resistant and easier to launder. You will have to weigh up the advantages of ease of care against the disadvantages of not using a totally natural product.

Buying natural fibres is not always as ecologically sound as we might think. Many cotton and linen growers use pesticides although there are organic cotton growers who use integrated pest management to control insects.

Cotton is usually bleached after harvesting and dyed and linen may be similarly treated, although it is far better bleached in natural sunlight. However it is possible to buy bed linens, bath towels and some curtain and loose-cover fabrics which are unbleached, undyed and untreated, so ask the supplier or manufacturer for the 'history' of the fabric. Unfortunately organically produced cotton and untreated natural fibres are likely to be more expensive.

WALL COVERINGS

Wallpaper is readily available and far more appropriate than a vinyl wall covering, which is actually printed onto a PVC sheet and then backed with paper, making an impervious wall surface that prevents the wall underneath from 'breathing'. Plastic wall coverings made from foamed polyethylene should be avoided. As yet I have not heard of a wall covering made from recycled paper but I am sure this will come soon. Meanwhile, natural brown and green wrapping paper, newspapers, even gift wrap and book endpapers can be used to decorate walls successfully. Or you might prefer to use paint on your walls, which can of course be put on over a lining or a wood-chip paper

PAINTS, STAINS AND FINISHES

Paint is probably one of the most useful materials for healing your home cosmetically. You can use it on walls, ceilings, floors, woodwork and metalwork. Highly versatile, paint comes in almost every colour you can think of. But you must use the right paint for the job. Some paints are only suitable for walls or ceilings, others are more appropriate for wood or metal.

Stains and varnishes are usually confined to wood furniture, to enhance the finish, bringing up the natural grain of the wood, or to produce a decorative treatment.

Check the contents of paints, primers and varnishes very carefully. Most paints once contained lead as a drying agent, now known to be poisonous. It is being phased out but check to ensure that your paint is lead-free. Older paintwork around your home may contain lead so replace it carefully.

Some paints and varnishes, particularly gloss finishes, may also contain solvents or other harmful chemicals and most are petrochemically based. A natural resin such as shellac, used as a varnish, and to prevent knots in wood showing through the top surface, is infinitely preferable to one containing polyurethane and can be used to seal bonded and other chemically treated buildings materials such as particleboard, chipboard, plywood or MDF.

There are other natural resin-based varnishes. Some organic paint manufacturers make a microporous varnish known as lazur which is user-friendly, does not emit fumes and is biodegradable. For exterior use, it has to be tinted with pigment to protect wood from ultraviolet rays but inside it can be used in its natural form.

There are organic oil-based paints, which can be used on wood, stone and metal, indoors and out. These are based on plant oils, resins and other natural ingredients. Colour is provided by adding pure earth pigments. Organic masonry paints are available for exterior stonework, stucco and pebbledash. Alternatively, you can use traditional limewash, tinted with natural pigments.

Most water-based paints such as distemper or emulsion are less likely to contain harmful ingredients but are only suitable for walls, and ceilings. They can be applied directly onto plaster, plasterboard or lining paper. Paint manufacturers are currently experimenting with water-based gloss paints that

can be used on woodwork and metal. There are organic wall emulsion paints, which usually come in white or a very limited range of colours, but you can colour them to your own recipe with natural pigments. Traditional distemper and milk (casein) paints are also made from natural ingredients; again, you can add the colour yourself.

Finally, if you have the time, you could make your own paints, which will give you the chance to create unique colours and finishes, and recipes are available. Water-based paints are easier to make: distemper, or limewash are mixed in a bucket with water, pigment is added and you are ready to go!

FURNITURE

Synthetic sealants or spray polishes for wooden furniture and surfaces frequently contain harmful chemicals; as aerosols, too, they make use of CFCs which damage the ozone layer. Avoid them. You can either use non-polluting alternatives or traditional products such as beeswax or natural oils. These are more eco-friendly and smell good. Linseed oil is often used to feed bare wood but can yellow the surface. Again, you can make your own furniture polish: turpentine mixed with linseed oil; olive oil with vinegar; or vegetable oil with lemon juice. Polishes such as these can also be used for wood floors.

Use one of the organic paints or eco-friendly stains or sealants to paint furniture. If you are stripping off a previous surface avoid caustic strippers, which can be highly toxic and also damaging. Sanding down wood is preferable but wear a face mask for safety while sanding.

Use natural fabrics or leather to upholster furniture. Avoid vinyl or PVC, which can cause various disorders. The ubiquitous plastic foam, which became popular some twenty years ago, is now known to be a serious fire hazard. Fumes given off from the smouldering foam are highly toxic and can be fatal. Avoid any furniture which contains this foam and remove any already in your house. Instead, use natural products for fillings such as flock (made from cotton waste), horsehair, wool, pure down or a feather and down mix. If somebody in your household is allergic to any of these, he or she could use a foam-rubber-filled mattress but ensure that there is a special barrier fabric covering the foam and under the top cover for fire retardancy. Pillows, quilts and duvets can be filled with cotton (like the mattresses on futons), foam rubber, or wool.

Today, new domestic upholstery has to pass a cigarette and match test for safety. Some natural fabrics, such as wool, may be inherently flame-retardant; fabrics can also be treated by back-coating or dipping but these products contain chemicals.

Encouraging sustainability

Most new kitchens, bathrooms or built-in bedrooms are made from what is known as medium-density fibreboard (MDF) or laminated boards, neither of which are particularly environmentally friendly. Natural wood is obviously healthier but if you are worried about threats to rain- or other forests, you can stipulate wood from quick-growing sustainable sources. Some environmentally aware kitchen and other furniture specialists even promise to plant a tree for every kitchen or bedroom they install so helping to replenish natural resources. If you are concerned about the over-use of natural materials, ask suppliers about their policy on 'plundering the planet' and follow your conscience. Friends of the Earth and other conservation and environmental groups will give advice and recommend manufacturers and stockists.

Using natural wood in your home is certainly healthier, but does pose an environmental dilemma; if you are at all worried, look for manufacturers who pledge to replenish the trees that they use.

HOME SAFE HOME

THE HEALTHY HOME should be a safe home. Every year literally thousands of people suffer accidents, some fatal, because their homes are poorly organized or designed. Common accidents include: scalding or burning from unguarded fires or cooking utensils; falls or trips because of awkwardly placed furniture, poor lighting or badly fitting carpets; cuts or other injuries from sharp implements or rough surfaces; and general bumping and bruising. Poisoning and electrical accidents are also common.

However, most accidents in the home can be avoided by taking simple precautions.

All toxic or poisonous substances from disinfectants through to decorating materials and medicines should be kept safely locked away. Cutting implements too from knives to gardening tools should always be stored safely.

In the kitchen, potentially one of the most dangerous rooms in the house, make sure that hot pans are guarded and cannot be pulled over. To avoid the risk of fire, keep a fire blanket close to the stove and invest in fire extinguishers that can be strategically placed through the home in case of need.

Tall houses need an outside fire escape. If you live in an apartment block, check the fire exits and make sure fire doors are always accessible and free from clutter. You can also buy special rope ladders, which can be thrown down from upper windows in case of an emergency. Think about the risk of fire and work out a suitable drill. Keep corridors and doors free of clutter for easy access into and out of rooms.

Glass and glazing are a feature of most houses. However, make sure that all windows can be opened easily in case of an emergency.

Good lighting is essential. A house that is well lit during the day and night should be accident-free. Make sure that dark corners, the insides of deep cupboards, stair treads and changes of level, inside and out-of-doors, are immediately visible. Also light front and back doors, house names and numbers.

Keep electrical equipment well maintained and switched off when not in use. Use circuit breakers outdoors and lock away specialist or expensive equipment.

Make sure that all floors are non-slip. If you use rugs, make sure they are secure and not liable to slipping or creeping. Check and maintain all carpets to ensure that they are in good condition. Deal immediately with any holes or ravels. Stair carpets are particularly vulnerable.

Furniture and fittings should stand firm, level and four-square, and not be in danger of toppling over. Check shelves and brackets regularly. Avoid furniture with sharp corners.

Cots, play pens and other children's furniture should be designed for safety and free from toxic paints. Use non-flammable and natural materials for sofas, chairs and other furniture.

Water features should be planned with care, particularly if there are young children about.

Security is an important aspect of safety. Consult a specialist for advice and use a professional to fit locks, window bolts and other security devices according to your personal needs.

Finally, keep a comprehensive first-aid kit conveniently to hand. Keep a list of emergency numbers by the telephone.

DIY Safely
Think health and safety when doing any **DIY**. Work in dry, well-ventilated areas and protect yourself if using toxic materials. Keep tools well maintained and wear a face mask and goggles if sanding floors or cutting glass or ceramics. Work at a bench, using a vice to grip items. Keep paints, stains and varnishes well sealed.

You can introduce quite simple precautions to make your home a safer place.

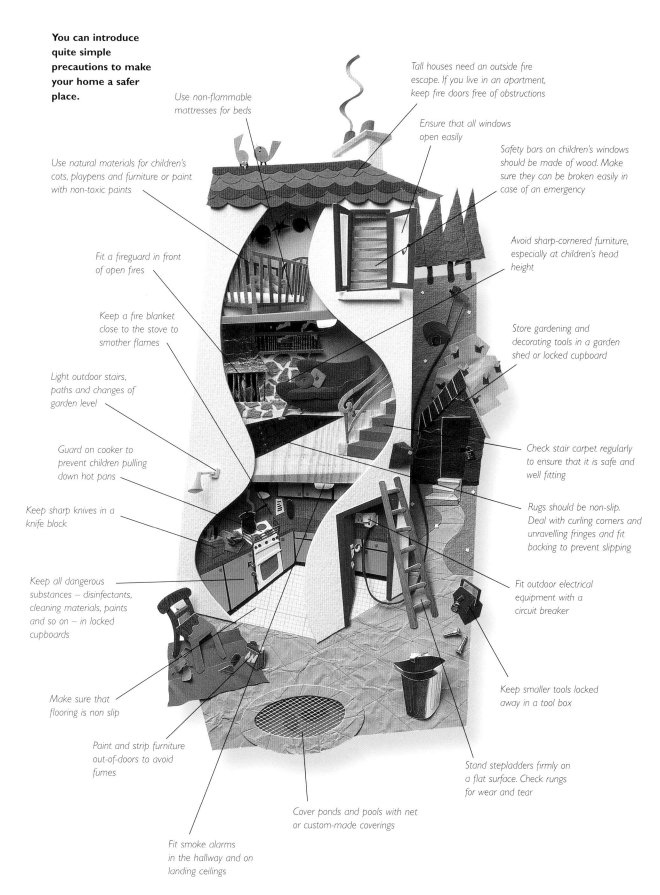

Use non-flammable mattresses for beds

Tall houses need an outside fire escape. If you live in an apartment, keep fire doors free of obstructions

Ensure that all windows open easily

Safety bars on children's windows should be made of wood. Make sure they can be broken easily in case of an emergency

Use natural materials for children's cots, playpens and furniture or paint with non-toxic paints

Fit a fireguard in front of open fires

Avoid sharp-cornered furniture, especially at children's head height

Keep a fire blanket close to the stove to smother flames

Store gardening and decorating tools in a garden shed or locked cupboard

Light outdoor stairs, paths and changes of garden level

Guard on cooker to prevent children pulling down hot pans

Check stair carpet regularly to ensure that it is safe and well fitting

Keep sharp knives in a knife block

Rugs should be non-slip. Deal with curling corners and unravelling fringes and fit backing to prevent slipping

Keep all dangerous substances – disinfectants, cleaning materials, paints and so on – in locked cupboards

Fit outdoor electrical equipment with a circuit breaker

Make sure that flooring is non slip

Keep smaller tools locked away in a tool box

Paint and strip furniture out-of-doors to avoid fumes

Stand stepladders firmly on a flat surface. Check rungs for wear and tear

Cover ponds and pools with net or custom-made coverings

Fit smoke alarms in the hallway and on landing ceilings

HEALING WITH FENG SHUI

Feng shui can be used in many ways to enhance the health of your home and your general wellbeing. At the outset you can use the principles of feng shui to plan the purpose, layout and contents of your rooms in the most favourable ways. But you can also use feng shui to 'cure' existing faults that may be causing energy problems. Most cures involve the use of healthy plants, mirrors and light and offer simple and inexpensive ways of increasing favourable chi into the home. You can do them yourself or, if problems are severe, ask a feng shui consultant for advice.

Growing plants both indoors and out can do much to improve energy flows. Placed on the front doorstep or to each side of a path, they provide welcome and prevent energy from flowing out of the home. Staggered plants in the hallway also slow down fast-moving chi. Placed in the kitchen or the work room, plants also help to counteract radiation emissions. Spiky plants too, such as yuccas, can prevent stagnant chi from gathering in a corner.

Corners thrusting into a room or angular-shaped furniture are said to create harmful cutting chi, 'poison arrows'. This can be softened and deflected by standing a large plant in front of the offending corner, or by trailing a plant over it. A fabric curtain has much the same effect. L-shaped rooms too cause energy imbalance and can be corrected by placing a mirror at the narrow point to increase a sense of space.

Neighbouring buildings can also cause cutting chi if a sharp corner points towards your home. Planting bushes or trees near the front door or placing reflective surfaces near the front door to deflect the chi will solve the problem.

Exposed structural beams are also likely to cause cutting or negative chi, especially if they are made of steel or concrete. In a high-ceilinged room the negative effects are weakened but using uplighters or tall leafy plants reduces the effect.

Internal corners can cause stagnant chi so speed up the energy by reflecting light from glossy-leaved plants, shiny textures or mirrors. Good lighting and pleasant sounds will also keep energy flowing.

Warnings:
Never position mirrors opposite each other as energy will bounce from one to the other.

Do not put mirrors opposite a door or window as this will reflect back energy entering the room.

Avoid mirrors, or mirror tiles, that distort the body.

Light and freedom from clutter are both integral to the feng shui philosophy. Too much clutter can cause stagnation, so organize your possessions well, put things away tidily and have a major throw-out and reorganization occasionally. Use daylight bulbs and kinetic lighting to bring light into dark areas.

MIRRORS
Mirrors often provide simple solutions. They speed up and redirect the flow of energy and light waves, magnifiyng light and creating an impression of greater space. Shiny metal, reflective glass, highly polished furniture and glazed ceramic tiles can all have the same effect.

Circular mirrors reflect chi energy in several directions, spreading it out and helping to disperse fast-moving or cutting chi. Flat mirrors reflect in just one direction. Octagonal mirrors are particularly significant, their eight sides reflecting the eight directions of the compass. Low, wide, rectangular-shaped mirrors create a stable, calm atmosphere; tall, thin rectangular mirrors encourage upward moving energy.

Careful positioning of mirrors helps to move chi harmoniously through the home. If you have a long, narrow corridor or hall, slow energy down by positioning staggered mirrors on opposite walls. If stairs face the front door, there is a danger that chi will disappear out of the house; place a large, flat mirror next to the front door to reflect energy back into the house. To be most effective, mirrors should be sparkling clean.

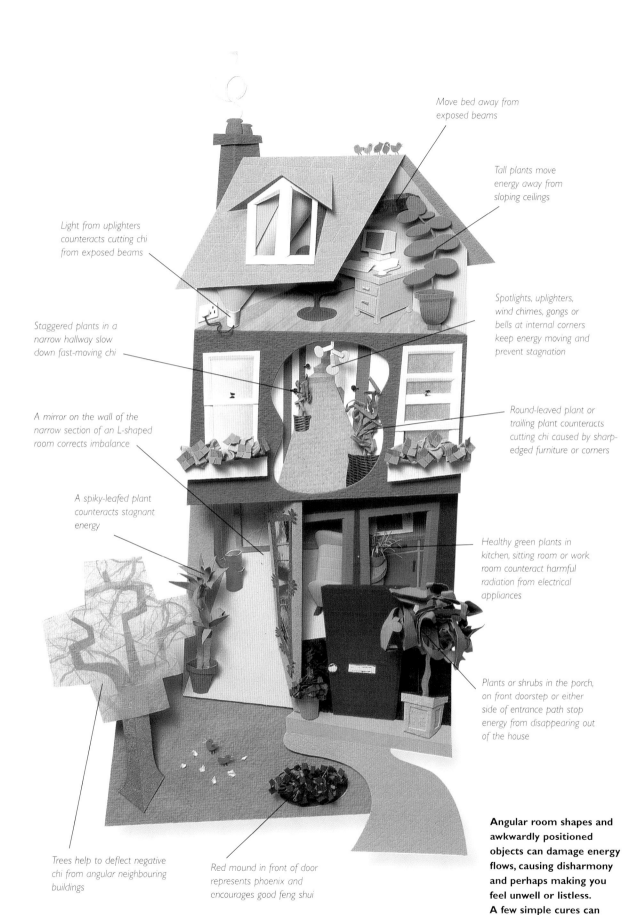

Move bed away from exposed beams

Tall plants move energy away from sloping ceilings

Light from uplighters counteracts cutting chi from exposed beams

Staggered plants in a narrow hallway slow down fast-moving chi

Spotlights, uplighters, wind chimes, gongs or bells at internal corners keep energy moving and prevent stagnation

A mirror on the wall of the narrow section of an L-shaped room corrects imbalance

Round-leaved plant or trailing plant counteracts cutting chi caused by sharp-edged furniture or corners

A spiky-leafed plant counteracts stagnant energy

Healthy green plants in kitchen, sitting room or work room counteract harmful radiation from electrical appliances

Plants or shrubs in the porch, on front doorstep or either side of entrance path stop energy from disappearing out of the house

Trees help to deflect negative chi from angular neighbouring buildings

Red mound in front of door represents phoenix and encourages good feng shui

Angular room shapes and awkwardly positioned objects can damage energy flows, causing disharmony and perhaps making you feel unwell or listless. A few simple cures can heal the problems.

169

HEALING A HOME

SECOND TIME AROUND

WE HAVE AT LAST WOKEN up to the dreadful vandalism perpetrated on buildings and houses in the name of progress during the first sixty years of the 20th century. Today the trend is towards preserving our heritage, protecting or restoring buildings and architectural features, in some cases completely restoring a property to its original architectural style and glory. Conversions too, such as factory and warehouse conversions into living spaces, are now done in a more sympathetic way, with greater consideration for the overall look and its place in the local environment.

Fortunately many traditional building materials and architectural items, such as windows, doors, plasterwork, fireplaces, stoves, cornices, mouldings and panelling, have been saved and are still available for reuse. There are also many builder's yards that specialize in salvaged and recycled products. Increasingly too there is an army of people who are training in traditional crafts and can help with restoration of wood, plaster, stone and even thatching. Some are involved in prestigious projects, restoring historic buildings such as London's Westminster Abbey; others are available to help designers, architects and home owners on less complex projects.

However, before you rush to call in an expert, it is well worthwhile looking carefully at your home to see how much of the original structure still exists, perhaps hidden away behind plasterboard, tiling or fitted carpets. Floors made from terracotta *carres*, flagstones, slate, inlaid parquet, quarry or encaustic tiles may well be hiding under a layer or two of linoleum, vinyl, or underfelt and fitted carpet. If you don't want this type of flooring, or any other original feature you may discover hidden away, don't destroy it; have it taken up, or out, very carefully by a salvage expert so it can be reused in a different area of your home, or by somebody else. Your 'white elephant' may be someone

One of the starting points for an eco-friendly home is to reuse or restore wherever possible. Before you rush out to buy, take a careful look at your own home. You may find that behind an old piece of plasterboard is a beautiful fireplace.

Always check old wood for woodworm before reusing it and bringing it into your home.

else's source of enjoyment, and may bring you some extra cash.

On the other hand, if you do want interesting architectural features, or a traditional floor, you should be able to find suitable materials and old floorings and have them relaid in your home. Some of the rich terracotta tiles, golden flagstones and subtle slates have been reclaimed from old French chateaux, or Tuscan farmhouses, for instance, and have a wonderfully warm quality and a patina of age which makes them a joy to live with.

If you want wooden floors, you may be able to restore, repair, strip, sand and seal existing floorboards. If they are very worn, painted or heavily stained, you can take them up, turn them over and relay them, effectively creating new boards that will have the advantage of being cut to size and shape as well as being well seasoned.

Such restoration is only practical if you are planning a fair bit of rebuilding because it will involve structural work such as removing skirtings, repairing joists and replastering. However, once you have your new surface, you can decorate it to taste: stencilling, marbelling or even handpainting.

SALVAGING AND RECYCLING
Reusing salvaged items may not necessarily mean restoring the fabric of your own home. Enterprising designers, furniture specialists, carpenters and manufacturing companies are making new furniture, accessories, sculptures and other decorative

An increasing number of designers and furniture-makers are producing furniture and fittings made from recycled furniture, which you can buy. If appropriate, you can also strip surfaces back to reveal original brickwork and beams.

artefacts from recycled materials such as old beams and panelling, driftwood or disused railway sleepers, all of which can take on a new lease of life converted into tables, benches and cupboards. Old, heavy and unattractive pieces of furniture can also be dismantled (originally many of them were built to come apart easily) and re-shaped as several smaller items.

I once bought an enormous Victorian mahogany and satinwood wardrobe, sitting on a base of two large drawers, with two storage cupboards to each side, and a set of drawers and small cupboards in the centre, all joined by a heavy carved cornice on top. I took it to pieces and made a seat and a toy store from the base, used the cornice to make a decorative window pelmet,

reused the cupboards as part of a non-fitted kitchen and still use the drawers and cupboard for storage and filing in my study.

Some designers specialize in trawling roadside skips and local 'dumping' sites, converting well-seasoned timbers, malleable metal or other pliant materials into useful household items, or eye-catching art forms. There is no reason why you should not join this band of creative magpies, although it is, of course, only good manners to ask the household or builder if you can take something out of their skip.

Other hunting grounds for recyclable materials include forests or woodlands, where branches and trees may have fallen in a storm, seashores, canals and river banks. Driftwood can be converted into doors, tables, chairs, kitchen furniture and so on or crafted into models and sculptures. It can also be a decorative accessory in its own right, particularly when combined with indoor plants. Larger pieces, which may have been left stranded by the tide or discovered half-buried in mud, can be used for furniture. Many rustic garden benches, for instance, began life as something different.

Recycling need not be confined to the reuse of wood and metal. Small scraps of fabric can be recycled for herb pillows, or stitched into patchwork for quilts and cushions or pegged or plaited into rag rugs. Antique textiles, too, such as pieces of tapestry, embroidery , old lace or velvet can be converted into cushions, table covers, lamp shades and other accessories.

Many textiles and rugs can be used as decorative wall hangings, and I have seen some damaged Kilim rugs cut down and used for upholstery for stools, small chairs and floor cushions. There are experts who specialize in this sort of work but these are crafts that you can learn to do yourself. Furniture too can be given a new lease of life by mending or reupholstering, again crafts you can learn and that bring great satisfaction.

Many household items, from glass bottles and jars through to plastic containers can also be recycled for use in your own home, perhaps as storage jars or plant or candle holders. Paper too can be recycled creatively within your house rather than being taken to a paper bank. Papier mâché, made from torn or shredded paper bound with flour-and-water paste, is easy to make, and can be used for a variety of objects. The Victorians,

The number of businesses dealing in salvaged materials from old properties has increased in the past few years. They provide a happy hunting ground for beautiful old tiles and even larger items such as a kitchen range.

Reduce, reuse and recycle are the three **Rs** of resource consciousness. Much household waste – paper, cans, glass, food – can be recycled. But recycling is not an end in itself. We should also reduce consumption and reuse whatever we can.

for instance, used papier mâché for making furniture, trays, bowls, decorative plates and paintings. In some cases they inlayed the objects with mother of pearl. It has even been used for buildings; a Norwegian church, for instance, has been built from paper that was recycled in this way.

Old ceramic tiles can be recycled to create a 'patchwork' wall or floor, using flooring grade tiles. Alternatively, broken pieces can be used to make decorative mosaics in bathrooms and kitchens or to convert ordinary flower pots, window boxes and tubs into more decorative containers.

Glass too can be recycled for decorative use, perhaps cut and leaded into 'stained' glass panels. Broken car windscreen glass, which has dull edges, has also been recycled creatively. Combined with gravel, it can give added glitter to a path or patio.

RECYCLING WASTE

It has been estimated that at least 80 per cent of all our household rubbish could be recycled. This includes paper, glass, food waste, cans and clothing. And these days most local authorities or supermarkets provide a range of recycling facilities.

Appropriately enough my local authority provides green containers for unwanted glass bottles, jars, cans, paper and fabrics, which then are collected weekly.

But as well as recycling and reusing, you should also aim to reduce consumption in order to avoid generating yet more waste. Try not to buy too much pre-packaged food and other products. Reuse plastic carrier bags or ask for paper bags, which can be recycled, in preference to plastic and other non-degradable packaging. Buy drinks, milk, cosmetics and other products in glass containers rather than plastic. Invest in a water purifier and soda stream so that you can make your own drinks. Try making your own wine, jams, chutneys and preserves as well, remembering to recycle the containers each time.

Recycle all kitchen or food waste. If you live in a rural area you may be able to give some to a nearby farm for animal food, or even keep and feed your own livestock such as ducks, geese or chickens. If this is not possible, turn your food scraps into compost for use in your garden.

Sort household waste carefully; separating the various types of waste is crucial to any successful recycling programme. Separate and store waste in one place, ideally close to the kitchen or in a utility area or garage where it will remain dry. Use separate bins for different kinds of waste, perhaps colour coded for recognition. They should be handy for collection or transportation to a recycling site. Rinse glass bottles, jars and cans. If you are recycling aluminium foil containers, rinse these too before taking them to the recycling centre. Hazardous waste such as old batteries, plastics, paint, paint thinners and other caustic liquids should be sealed and disposed of safely, perhaps in a landfill.

Large metal and aluminium items, old household appliances and furniture can also be recycled and reused. You could give them directly to a charity or arrange for collection by the relevant authority or specialist collector. Organizations such as Friends of the Earth can usually advise.

HEALTHY HOUSEKEEPING

A HEALTHY HOME should be clean and free of clutter. But an exhausted housekeeper and children being continually nagged not to make a mess is not conducive to healthy living. An over-clean home can be very sterile so aim for a healthy compromise between hygiene and comfort.

As well as using healthy materials to decorate and furnish your home, you should use 'friendly' and healthy products to clean it. Many eco-friendly cleaning products are available today but you can also use various environmentally friendly methods used by our grand- and great grandmothers.

CLEANING AND WASHING MATERIALS

Many of these are environmental hazards. Washing powders and liquids contain bleaching agents or detergents that can irritate the skin, possibly causing allergic reactions. Long-term they can also destroy fibres in textiles causing fabrics to rot, wear out and loose colour.

When these cleaners are flushed away, the water-polluting phosphates take a long time to break down, causing problems to both fish and plant life.

The alternative is to use some of the now widely available phosphate-free biodegradable products. These include washing-up liquids, fabric conditioners and clothes washing liquids, powders and conditioners. Containing natural oils and plant extracts, they are non-polluting and non-irritating.

You can also freshen and soften your clothes by adding 1 teaspoonful of white vinegar or bicarbonate of soda to the final rinse. And there is no better way of achieving fresh-smelling linens and clothes than by hanging them out to dry naturally in the air and sunshine – and you will save energy. For washing dishes, you can use plain, pure soap, adding a little lemon juice or white vinegar if there is grease to contend with.

BLEACHES AND SCOURING POWDERS

or other 'dirt-busting' liquids are also hazardous – have you noticed how advertisements frequently suggest an army of strong men is helping to rid your home of dirt with the muscle power contained in their particular product? These products contain chlorine compounds, which give off toxic fumes that irritate both skin and surfaces. Bleach burns the skin, is highly toxic if swallowed and damages fabric. Some scouring powders and cleansers contain ammonia. If

Bleaches and detergents damage the skin and cause long-term harm to the environment. You can replace them with ready-made eco-friendly products or make your own cleaners using vinegar, horsetail and bicarbonate of soda.

Vinegar

Horsetail

Bicarbonate of soda

Bleaches

Corrosive cleaners

Salt

Soda

Foil

Silver cutlery

Most metal cleaners are corrosive. You can clean cutlery with an environmentally friendly mixture of salt, water, soda and silver foil.

bleach or lavatory cleansers, are mixed with other ammonia-containing substances, they will give off chloramine gas, which pollutes water and destroys the bacteria that break down sewage.

General purpose biodegradable cleaners are available but you can also make your own healthy cleaners with bicarbonate of soda. Make this into a paste and leave on a dirty surface for a few minutes before rinsing off or just use neat on a damp sponge. Fine wood ash and horsetail (a wild plant) is also a good natural scourer. And you can pour white vinegar into the lavatory bowl and leave it overnight to freshen, cleanse and whiten. Use a mild borax or tea tree oil solution to disinfect.

FLOOR, FURNITURE AND METAL POLISHES can also give off

fumes or cause skin irritation. In their aerosol form they discharge particles of chemical solvents into the air, to say nothing of being ozone-damaging if the propellant contains CFCs. Metal polishes can also be highly corrosive and poisonous. Spray-on polish leaves a deposit on the surface of furniture, which eventually causes it to cloud and it may then have to be stripped and refinished.

Instead of these, use natural furniture polishes, such as beeswax, mixtures of oil and lemon or

vinegar, which will give your furniture a rich patina. Carnuba wax can be used for floors or they can be sealed with a 'button polish' made from a natural resin. Buff occasionally with a mop but don't make the surface too wet. Wooden floors need 'feeding' but other floors, such as linoleum or sealed cork, do not; an occasional mop with soapy water, rinsed off with fresh water will be enough.

You can also make your own cleaner for metals such as silver. Put a sheet of aluminium foil or some old foil tops and containers into a pan, cover with about 5–7 cm (2–3 ins) of water, add 1 teaspoonful salt and 1 teaspoonful bicarbonate of soda, or 1 tablespoon of washing soda, and bring to the boil. Drop in small items of silver cutlery and boil for about 3 minutes. Remove them and rinse, then buff with chamois leather or a soft duster. You can also use a powder made into a paste called jeweller's rouge. To clean very small items or delicate items of jewellery you can use toothpaste or surgical spirit applied with a paint or toothbrush. You can make

A cut lemon dipped in salt cleans most kitchen surfaces; boiling gooseberries scours the pan, and vinegar cleans toilets and baths.

a pot of 'dip-in' cleaner for small items of jewellery or fork tines by shredding foil to half fill a screw top jar. Add a tablespoon of salt, top up with water, shake and leave to steep. Pop in small items for about 2–3 minutes, rinse, dry and buff with a duster.

NATURAL GENERAL CLEANERS There are many

ways of cleaning with natural products such as bicarbonate of soda or lemons, all of them more user-friendly than spray-on caustic solutions. A lemon cut in half and dipped in salt will clean copper, brass, work surfaces, chopping boards or the inside of a microwave oven. Vinegar will remove limescale from the bath, lavatory and kettles, and can be used to clean mirrors and windows (buff them afterwards with a pad of old newspaper) and to bleach marble surfaces. Stains can be removed from metal saucepans with cream of tartar or by cooking rhubarb or gooseberries in them.

Vinegar

Gooseberries

Lemon

Cream of tartar

CONSERVING ENERGY

WE ARE NOW WELL AWARE of the urgent need to conserve resources such as energy and water. On a day-to-day basis this can be done in quite simple ways, such as switching off lights when they are not needed, using energy-saving or low-voltage bulbs or turning the heating thermostat down a notch or two. Measures such as these not only reduce energy consumption, they will also reduce your bills by as much as 40–60 per cent.

Other energy-conservation measures, such as roof or floor insulation, lagging hot-water tanks, or installing double glazing, may be more complex to install and will involve an initial financial outlay. But they too help to conserve valuable resources and will eventually pay for themselves.

Fossil fuels such as coal and oil are being rapidly depleted; other sources of energy such as nuclear-generated electricity carry their own environmental risks. Most of us, however, use electricity or gas for home needs, so in order to minimize consumption we need to consider the most efficient ways of using them.

As a general rule, electricity is most efficient for high-grade energy needs such as light and powering home and work appliances; while gas, oil and some solid fuels such as coal, anthracite or coke, are best kept for space and water heating.

CHOOSING AND USING APPLIANCES
Choose a really well-designed system that will provide heat for cooking, heating and water. You can base this on an energy-efficient stove, which will heat water and act as a range cooker. Alternatively, use a wood, gas- or coal-fired stove, possibly in a central fireplace, combined with a back boiler which will heat water and supply warmth to a few radiators. The stove doors can be opened to provide further radiant heat. Installation may be costly and involve structural work but is well worth considering if you are moving into a new home, or making major alterations to your existing home. If you are re-designing your kitchen, for instance, get rid of the conventional boiler and cooker and replace them with a range-cooker which will perform various functions, including drying clothes.

When buying new household appliances such as a washing machine or dishwasher, choose those with energy-saving features such as economy cycles. Remember to use these appliances only when they are full; by doing so, you will actually use less water and heat than when hand washing. You can also save energy by switching off a dishwasher once it reaches the drying cycle, opening the door, pulling out the shelves and letting the dishes dry in the warm air. Try to choose appliances that can be filled from your hot-water supply rather than using their own heater.

To save energy, dry clothes in the open air whenever possible, perhaps using the spin cycle or spin dryer to remove excess moisture or use drying racks that can be placed near radiators or sources of radiant heat.

It is up to you to decide how many appliances you want, or need. Think carefully before buying and using too many electrical appliances, and perhaps

Drying clothes in the open air avoids using electricity.

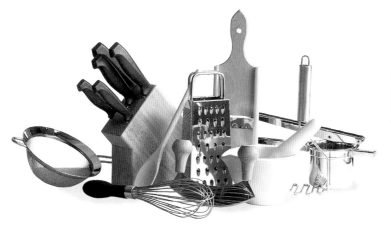

Hand-held kitchen equipment – sharp knives, a grater, a whisk, a sieve and pestle and mortar – can easily replace electrical appliances.

reassess how often you really need to use them. Do you really need to use a vacuum cleaner every day? A simple damp or dry mopping or a run over with a carpet sweeper is a good energy-saving compromise. Let your hair dry naturally rather than using a hair-dryer. If appropriate use a hob kettle rather than an electric one. Look at kitchen appliances critically. Most kitchens have electrical gadgets tucked away in a corner, gathering dust and never used. Reassess the situation; only keep what you actually use. Balloon whisks, wooden spoons, sharp cooking knives, a grater, mandolin slicer, and hand-operated vegetable 'ricer' can chop and blend food just as efficiently as any electric mixer.

Save energy when you are cooking. Only the fill the kettle with the water you need. Don't use the grill for a single piece of toast. Develop the art of slow cooking with electric slow cookers, which use very little energy. Cook several items from one energy source. For instance use a tiered steamer over one flame or hot plate to cook fish or meat, potatoes and other vegetables all at the same time. Put lids on saucepans and turn the heat down once the contents have boiled. Use a heat diffuser to spread the flame for slow simmering; turn off electric cookers or hobs before the food is completely cooked – the remaining heat will complete the process. Fan settings on an oven will use less energy than conventional settings, as cooking times will be shorter and temperatures slightly lower. Pressure cookers too can be used to cook several items of food at once. And if you are cooking small quantities use a microwave.

Use your oven efficiently too. Try to cook several dishes at the same time; you might be cooking a main dish, and vegetables but also cook some fruit (fresh or dried) or pulses, jacket potatoes, a milk pudding or stock to serve later. If you are buying a new cooker, consider one which has two ovens – a smaller one for everyday use and fewer dishes and a larger one for family and celebratory meals. A griddle pan is often a more economical and healthy way of cooking food.

At the other end of the heat scale, use your refrigerator economically – it is unnecessary to have a giant all-singing, all-dancing, all-cooling monster in the corner! If you have a cool larder or food cupboard it is often much better to keep all but the most perishable food in this. Sometimes a food cupboard or 'meat safe' can be placed in a cool, shady place outside, against a north-facing wall, with a well-ventilated wire grille instead of doors.

If you are buying a new fridge or freezer, the chest type is more economical than the pull-out drawer type. Check for energy efficiency and that it has a non-CFC coolant. Defrost fridges regularly for efficiency and ideally position freezers or fridges on an outside, preferably north, wall away from the boiler, stove or cooker. Site a freezer in a utility room, outhouse or garage. Freezers work more efficiently if they are full. This does not mean you have to rush out to buy frozen items or prepare fresh food for freezing; you can fill spaces with loaves of bread or even clean towels.

Service all appliances regularly so they operate as efficiently as possible. Keep larger items such as washing machines, boilers, and heaters well ventilated and clear of dust, animal hairs and food; a clogged system may have to work twice as hard so using greater amounts of energy.

To save energy, consider using a multi-layered steamer so that you can cook three courses or dishes at the same time.

INSULATION Adequate insulation also helps to conserve energy by minimizing heat loss. The amount of work you need to carry out will very much depend on your particular home: a flat, terraced house or semi-detached property is always warmer than a separate building because of the number of walls in common with the neighbouring property. You also need to consider climate, prevailing winds, shade and the orientation of your home.

Methods of insulation include lagging water pipes and cold tanks, insulating a loft, putting a 'jacket' on the hot-water tank, and insulating exterior walls either with cavity insulation or external or internal insulation to solid walls. You can also insulate basement and ground floors and double-glaze windows to reduce heat loss. You can do many simple insulation jobs yourself – lagging pipes, installing draught excluders – but others are more complex and you will need professional assistance.

Building a glazed porch onto a front or back door, or adding a conservatory or sun room to your home also cuts down on draughts and traps sunlight, creating a solar energy conservator.

If you have conventional central heating, the positioning of radiators is important. It is more efficient to place radiators against an internal wall, rather than under a window, allowing heat to disappear outside. Windows and their frames should be draughtproof, to prevent cold air from entering. Place reflective foil on the wall behind the radiator to reflect heat and, if you wish, place a shelf or sill above the radiator to deflect hot air. Radiator covers can be elegant but cut the warm air flow – better to disguise a radiator by painting it to blend in with its background. Fit radiators with thermostats to conserve energy.

Draughtproofing is a good, cheap and easy form of insulation. Put draught strips on ill-fitting doors and windows, using a metallic strip rather than adhesive foam,

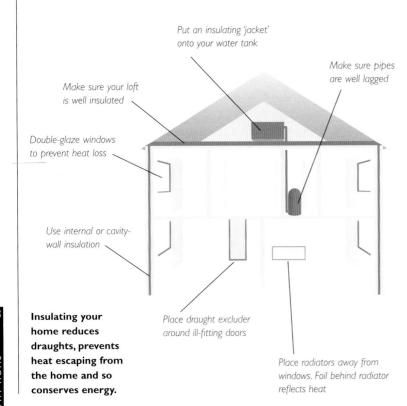

Put an insulating 'jacket' onto your water tank

Make sure pipes are well lagged

Make sure your loft is well insulated

Double-glaze windows to prevent heat loss

Use internal or cavity-wall insulation

Place draught excluder around ill-fitting doors

Place radiators away from windows. Foil behind radiator reflects heat

Insulating your home reduces draughts, prevents heat escaping from the home and so conserves energy.

Lighting efficiency tips

■ switch lights off when you are not using them

■ use a dimmer switch to control light and reduce use of power

■ use low-wattage bulbs where small amounts of light are appropriate

■ invest in low-energy bulbs; compact fluorescent bulbs, for instance, last about 8,000 hours each as opposed to 1,000 hours of the regular type. The Worldwatch Institute calculates that every compact fluorescent bulb you use saves 180kg of coal and keeps 130kg of carbon out of the atmosphere

■ use tungsten-halogen bulbs, they last twice as long as regular filament bulbs

■ use a timer for security lighting, adjusting weekly as the daylight changes, or choose an automatic system, triggered when someone approaches. Timers will also control room heaters, water heaters and boilers.

A water butt in the garden collects water from gutters and downpipes, which can be used to water lawns, plants and your hair.

which disintegrates. You can also place draught excluders against the bottom of the doors. The traditional Victorian draught excluder – a door curtain made from heavy chenille drape mounted on a special *portiere* rod - is also worth considering for living-room doors.

Insulate or draughtproof floors, without structural work, by using thick underfelt under carpets to reduce heat loss on ground or basement levels. Put foil or a thick underlayer under vinyls or other semi-permanent flooring. Cork tiles are natural insulators.

Windows are one of the main sources of heat loss. Double-glazing is a highly effective form of insulation but a layered treatment is also practical and a good insulator. To achieve this, fit shutters or insulating blinds close to the glass then add full-length lined curtains. Leave the curtains open during the day to let the sun's rays in, and close them as it begins to get dark.

Let as much sun into the house as possible; the more natural warmth and light you achieve, the less energy you will use.

Improve your heating systems by the use of a heat exchanger, also called a heat recovery ventilator (HRV). This ventilates and retains some of the heat from warm air as it leaves the house, passing it to the fresh air coming in. A specialist heating engineer will fit this to your existing system

SAVING WATER Thousands of gallons of water are washed and flushed away from every home daily, particularly in countries such

as the United States and Britain where householders tend to use water in a wasteful fashion. Water is a valuable resource; it needs conserving just as much as energy.

Make sure that all your taps and pipes are tight fitting and do not leak or drip. Install a shower with a low-flow shower head, either above the normal bath or above a special compact ship's or 'sitz' bath. Use the shower in preference to the bath unless you need to take a long soak. You might also want to save water by sharing your bath with a friend, or reusing the water for children.

In the lavatory, reduce the amount of water you flush away by installing a low-flushing cistern or by putting a brick or a marble-filled plastic container into the cistern. Make sure these do not interfere with any moving parts. Traditional suspended cisterns with a pull chain use less water than the low-level flush type, so you may like to consider one of these.

Get into the habit of turning off all taps. Don't run water down the plug while you brush your teeth, shave or wash. In the kitchen, clean vegetables and other food in a bowl of water and a colander rather than under a running tap. Then use the water on your plants. If you wash dishes by hand, use a small bowl of hot, soapy water, and a second, larger bowl with clean, hot water for rinsing.

Think carefully about how you use water outside. Install a rainwater butt in the garden to collect for lawns, plants and vegetables and softer water for hair washing. Recycle your bath and other household water and use this for plants – be sure you have used biodegradable, non-toxic soaps and cleaners. Sprinkler systems and hoses should be avoided. Watering cans are harder work but preferable. If you do use a hose, control the flow of water carefully and save it for precious plants or vegetables. You can conserve moisture by mulching vegetables and flower beds. Water the garden in the early morning or evening so that water does not evaporate too quickly.

As a long-term plan, you could reduce your lawn in favour of a patio, and plant water-conserving ground-creeper plants, shrubs and trees. Use shrubs, hedges and creeper- or vine-covered trellis to shade hot, dry areas from the sun. Choose hardy house plants that require little watering.

Save water by rinsing vegetables in a bowl rather than under a running tap.

INTRODUCING ALTERNATIVE ENERGY

Solar panels trap heat from the sun, which can be stored and distributed through the home for washing and heating. Panels such as these are effective even on cloudy days.

MOST HOMES TODAY are still connected to main services but there is an increasing move towards using so-called alternative, appropriate or renewable energy resources, namely sun, wind and water, and much research is going into making these more practical for domestic use. Renewable energy systems will involve an initial financial outlay, unless they are already installed into a new property, but in the long run they can not only reduce your heating and other energy costs dramatically but also make your home more self-sufficient and environmentally friendly.

The practicality of installing renewable systems does to some extent depend where your property is situated, although solar panels will work almost anywhere, even in a grimy city, provided they are correctly positioned. You will require a certain amount of space for wind-power machinery, a source of water if you want to sink a well, or harness water power.

SOLAR energy makes maximum use of the heat from the sun. In order to harness solar power to warm your home or heat your water you will need some specialist equipment and advice from an expert to ensure that you site any solar equipment heat exchanger or thermal storage correctly.

There are two types of solar heating: passive and active. In the first, the warmth of the sun is used to warm the interior of the house. The building is specifically designed to store heat and release it at night, or on cold and cloudy days; thermal 'storage' heaters work on the same principal. Fans may be necessary to circulate the heat. Passive solar systems are relatively inexpensive to install, especially if you are restructuring your home, or building a new one, and maintenance is minimal because there are no complicated structures or mechanical parts to go wrong or be serviced. However, it is rarely sufficient for all heating needs and may have to be backed up with more conventional forms of energy.

Wind is a clean, safe source of power and has been used for centuries. As yet its domestic use is limited because of cost and concern about the visual impact of wind farms.

The active system uses solar panels, made from glass or plastic covered metal 'collector' panels, sited on a sloping sun-facing roof, which absorb the heat from the sun, even on cloudy days, and store it in various ways for heating water or for whole house heating. As ducts, pipes, fans, pumps and valves are necessary to distribute heat, maintenance and servicing will be required, although there are systems which work on the principle of hot water rising – just as air does – so it will circulate through the system without having to be pumped. Again this type of heating may be used to 'top up' more conventional systems.

When you are planning the use of solar energy, remember the summer! You will be able to make maximum use of the longer hours of sunshine to heat water and for thermal storage for the cooler evenings/days, but it is essential that you consider adequate ventilation and cooling to avoid over-heating. It may be necessary to incorporate shading techniques, and to have special self-opening vents which work on a temperature or light sensor control.

Solar systems can also be used in greenhouses and conservatories both to bring on growing plants, and to 'trap' some extra heat for use in the home.

WIND AND WATER POWER

are also unlimited providers of energy and have been used for centuries – as windmills – to harness the wind and use it to drive machinery to grind corn, and other cereals for flour. Watermills have performed similar functions but rely on a fairly fast-flowing 'mill' stream.

Both sources can be harnessed to provide domestic power via wind and water generators, although at the moment these tend to be rather expensive and very sophisticated. The practicality of being able to use these alternatives really does depend on the location of a property. As anybody who has watched a raging torrent tearing down a mountainside knows, this type of awesome landscape might not be the right place to erect a home, even if it were possible to buy land and obtain permission to build.

Another point to keep in mind when using water as a source of energy – with global warming, more and more streams and rivers are drying to a trickle and, as cold winters become less frequent, there will be fewer mountain torrents resulting from melted snow, another reason for considering solar power. The water in the sea could also be used to drive turbines and generators but as yet this is not practical for the single user.

Wind power is dependent on the speed and the frequency of the wind. Desert- and sea-facing sites or rounded hilltops are often the most successful position for the modern version of the windmill – the wind generator, which still relies on traditional sails to power it. In order for this to be a really feasible option, several windmills would be necessary and research is being conducted into creating wind farms to harvest the wind power and supply it to communities. One concern is the despoiling of the landscape; an army of triangular metal mills marching across a hillside can be as intrusive as pylons, and they are noisy.

American architect Frank Lloyd Wright built Falling Water in Pennsylvania in the late 1930s. It remains a remarkable example of how the natural elements can be integrated into a dwelling.

GLOSSARY

A

ACCENT COLOUR – a colour added to a scheme to contrast, add interest and a 'lift'; can be provided in accessories added at the end of the redecorating/furnishing process

ACCESSORIES – small items such as pictures, cushions, china and glass, bath towels, statuary etc., added to a scheme to give it a personal touch (needs to relate to the style/function of room)

ACHROMATIC COLOURS – black, white and grey – pure neutrals devoid of hue (pure colour); added to a hue to create tonal variation

ANALOGOUS COLOURS – closely related colours, which create harmonious schemes; next to each other on a colour wheel

ARCHITECTURAL LIGHTING – light provided by fittings which are built into the main structure

ARCHITRAVE – frame (usually wood) round the outside of a door

B

BAUBIOLOGIE – 'building biology' – the (German/Scandinavian) principle of constructing healthy working and living environments based on an understanding of the relationship between the built environment and the health of people living or working in it

BIOCLIMATE – atmospheric conditions and processes affecting plant, animal and human biology

C

CACHE POT – a decorative container placed round a plant pot to conceal it/prevent water dripping onto a surface

CANDELA – measurement of luminous intensity equal to the brightness of one candle (approximately 12 lumens)

CFCs – Chlorofluorocarbons – propellant used in aerosols; used in refrigeration cooling etc

CHAISE LONGUE – low couch with one raised end, used as a day bed

CHI – Chi energy, which, according to Chinese philosophy, breathes life into the natural world, producing harmony, growth and wellbeing – in Feng Shui, the circulation of this energy is essential to a healthy home

CHROMA – measure of the intensity or saturation of a colour – a pure colour is high in chroma; a greyed or blackened one is low

CORNICE/COVING – decorative or curved plasterwork/wood which hides join between ceiling and wall

D

DADO/DADO RAIL – lower part of a wall, divided horizontally by the rail, usually decorated in a practical way to prevent damage to the wall surface; originally called a wainscoting; dado rail originally called a chair rail

DECORATIVE LIGHTING – Light fittings chosen to enhance the style of the room – often added as an accessory – lamp, pendants etc

DELFT RACK – shelf placed round the perimeter of a room at picture rail height to display china (originally blue Delftware)

DPC – damp-proof course installed as part of the foundations of a building to prevent rising damp

E

ECA – Electrical Contractors' Association

ELEVATION – flat plan of a wall drawn to scale showing features such as doors, windows in correct position, to scale

EPA – Environmental Protection Agency

F

FABRITRAK – patent system of fixing fabric to walls by means of a special track

FENG SHUI – Chinese philosophy blending astrology and geomancy, based on location affecting destiny; good Feng Shui situates buildings/arranges interiors to be in tune with nature and the universe to bring health, happiness and prosperity to inhabitants

FIBRE-OPTIC – light fittings incorporating bundles of fibres which move whilst the light appears at the tips of the fibre

FRAMING PROJECTOR – light fitting which enables the beam of light to be controlled; can also project light, shadows, colour on walls

FRIEZE – narrow horizontal area of wall between the cornice, coving or ceiling and the picture rail

G

GEOMAGNETIC FIELD – the earth's magnetic field; Geomagnetic Survey will establish the position of a property in relation to this

GROW LAMPS – lighting source designed to enhance plant growth

H

HRS/V – heat recycling system/ventilator

HUE – pure colour relating to the original colours of the spectrum which can be varied in chroma by the introduction of white, grey and black to lighten, deepen or enrich

HYDROSCOPIC – able to absorb moisture from the air (plants)

I

IEE – Institution of Electrical Engineers

INCIDENT LIGHT – light which a colour appears to reflect back which relates to its lightness or value (strength)

INDUCTIVE DIMMER – special form of dimmer which must be used if low-voltage lighting is to be dimmed

IR – Infrared

K

KELVIN – scale of measurement for the colour temperature of light

KINETIC LIGHTING – light provided by a moving source – candle or oil-lamp flame, open fire etc

L

LANTERN LIGHT – architectural feature when glazing is let into a void between ceiling and wall to light an area naturally – often used to light stairwells

LIGHTNESS (also VALUE) – amount of black, grey or white in a colour which determines its tonal value

LIVE PLASTER – plaster which is loose and may fall at any time – often caused by damp

LOAD-BEARING (wall) – a supporting wall, an integral part of the main structure of a building – its removal can cause the house to topple unless the load is supported by an RSJ

LOW ALLERGY HOUSE – house where dust-creating and dust-holding materials and chemicals outgassing are kept to a minimum

LUMENS – measure of light intensity designed as a unit of luminous flow from any one source

M

MDF – medium density fibreboard used in building construction and for furniture – gives off toxic fumes

MICROCLIMATE – a special individual climate which exists separately/is different from the surrounding area – often found in terrariums, bottle gardens etc

MICROWAVE – electromagnetic radiation used for fast cooking by energy absorption

N

NEUTRAL COLOURS – achromatic (colour-less) colours – black, white and grey are *True* neutrals; *Accepted* neutrals are creams, beiges, off-whites – often the colours of natural and undyed materials

NICEIC – National Inspection Council for Electric Installations

O

OUTGASSING – spontaneous release of gasses, both toxic and non-toxic as a material dries out or ages

P

PHOTOSYNTHESIS – process by which the energy of sunlight is trapped by chlorophyll in green plants and used to build up complex materials from carbon dioxide and water

POLYURETHANE – clear varnish/sealant derivative of plastic

PVC – Polyvinyl Chloride, used to create many plastic products and surfaces

R

R-VALUE – measure of material's resistance to heat loss or gain – the higher the R-value the greater the insulation capacity

RADON – a radioactive gas which is produced in the earth during the decaying process – can be present in many materials including granite

REFLECTIVE VALUE – the return of light waves from a surface differs, depending on its colour or texture, creating high, mid or low reflectance value – pale blues, yellows, yellow-greens have high reflective value; dark reds, blues and purples have low

RESILIENT FLOORING – the name given to semi-permanent flooring which is laid over the subfloor; usually flexible, washable and wear resistant eg. linoleum, cork, rubber

RSJ – rolled steel joist used to bear the weight of heavy loads; essential to strengthen building structure when a load-bearing wall has been partially or completely removed

S

SAD – Seasonally Affective Disorder – illness and depression brought about by lack of light during winter months – can be controlled by special SAD light sources

SATURATION – term used to describe the strength or vividness of a hue (colour) – high saturation indicates a pure colour; low saturation is a greyed/muted one

SHADE – technically a term used to define a degree of lightness; a pure colour mixed with black to deepen and enrich. In common usage, a colour differing slightly from a specified hue

SITZ/SHIPS' BATH – small space-saving bath which is used by the bather in the sitting position, often combined with a shower

SOLAR ENERGY – natural energy from the sun which can be trapped and used for heating, water heating, etc

STRUCTURAL LIGHTING – light fittings built into the main structure of a building (architectural lighting)

T

TASK LIGHTING – lighting used specifically to illuminate a work surface or area in order for tasks to be performed

TINT – a colour (hue) to which a large amount of white has been added to create a very pale value (sometimes termed a pastel colour) eg., a 'tinted' white

TONAL CONTRAST – different values of colour used in a decorating scheme to provide essential contrast and visual interest

TONAL VALUE – the gradations of one colour from light to dark, which is created by mixing white (to lighten); grey (to create a mid-tone) and black (to darken)

TONE – technically a term used to define the degree of lightness of a colour

TOXOCARA CANIS – a round worm transmitted in dog faeces which can cause illness and eye damage particularly in children; lawns and earth which have been used by dogs as a lavatory can remain contaminated for several years

TREATMENT – wall, floor, surface, window etc. – a word used to describe the finish on a surface, or the way a window is dressed

U

UPLIGHTERS – light fittings designed to throw light upwards – can be wall or floor mounted or floor standing

UV – ultraviolet (light)

V

VALUE – a synonym for the degree of lightness of a colour or tone – its strength or weight

VDU – visual display unit, eg., the screen of a computer or television set

VOLTAGE – LOW-VOLTAGE LIGHTING – a type of lighting where a transformer is necessary to reduce the mains voltage usually to 12 volts; the transformer can be an integral part of the fitting or a separate unit installed between the mains source and fitting

W

WALLWASHERS – light fittings, usually ceiling-mounted, designed to gently wash the walls of a room with light

Y

YIN AND YANG – polar energies which in Chinese philosophy are seen as YIN, passive and dark (feminine), and YANG, active and bright (masculine)

There are many organizations and retail outlets specializing in environmentally-friendly products or in providing advice on ways of achieving a healthy home. The following pages list a selection.

Eco-building and design

Association for Environment Conscious Building
Nant-y-Gareg Farm
Saron
Llandyful
Dyfed SA44 5EJ
tel: 01559 370908
Produce a directory of green building products and services

The Building Centre
26 Store Street
London WC1E 7BT
tel: 0897 161136
Advice on building products and suppliers

Building Research Establishment (BRE)
Garston
Watford WD2 7JR
tel: 01923 664000
fax: 01923 664010
Consultancy on healthy buildings

Construction Research Communications Ltd
151 Rosebery Avenue
London EC1R 4QX
Publish BRE material on various aspects of buildings such as indoor air quality; publications available to purchase

Construction Resources
16 Great Guildford Street
London SE1
tel: 0171 450 2211
Eco-builders, merchants; seminars and advice on special eco-building techniques

Ecological Design Association (EDA)
The British School
Slad Road
Stroud
Glos GL5 1QW
tel: 01453 765575
fax: 01453 759211
Professional organization that publishes *EcoDesign* magazine and offers referrals to ecological architects and designers, as well as workshops and lectures

Institute of Building Biology
16 Church Street
Saffron Walden
Essex CB10 1JW

London Hazards Centre
3rd Floor
Headland House
308 Grays Inn Road
London WC1X 8DS
tel: 0171 837 5605
Researches alternatives to various indoor environmental hazards, from VDU radiation to timber treatments

Energy: conservation and alternative

Bristol Energy Centre and the Centre for Sustainable Energy
The Create Centre
B-bond Warehouse
Smeaton Road
Bristol BS1 6XN
tel: 0117 9304097
Concentrates on energy saving and fuel poverty with draught-proofing team

Centre for Alternative Technology
Llwyngwern Quarry
Machynlleth
Powys SY20 9AZ
tel: 01654 702400
Send £1 and a large SAE for their extensive mail-order booklet

Domestic Paraphernalia Co
Unit 15
Marine Business Centre
Dock Road
Lytham
Lancs FY8 5JA
tel: 01253 736 334

Energy Efficiency Service
Department of the Environment
Room 312 Thames House South
Millbank
London SW1P 6AA

Energy Research Group
Open University
Walton Hall
Milton Keynes MK7 6AA

The Energy Saving Trust
11-12 Buckingham Gate
London SW1E 6LB
tel: 0171 931 8401

Intermediate Technology Development Group
103-105 Southampton Row
London WC1B 4HH
tel: 0171 436 9761

Neighbourhood Energy Action
St Andrew's House
90-92 Pilgrim Street
Newcastle upon Tyne NE1 6SG
tel: 0191 261 5677
Promotes energy efficiency to combat fuel poverty

Practical Alternatives
Tir Gaia Solar Village
Rhayader
Powys LD6 5DX
tel: 01597 810929
Markets practical and durable goods
to help conserve Earth's resources

Solar Energy Unit
University College
Newport Road
Cardiff CF1 1TA

Recycled products and salvage

Architectural Salvage Centre
30-32 Stamford Road
London N1
tel: 0171 923 0783

LASSCo Flooring
Maltby Street
Bermondsey
London SE1
tel: 0171 237 4488
Reclaimed York stone flags,
limestone, old marble tiles and
cobbles

LASSCo RBK
101 Britannia Walk
London N1
tel: 0171 336 8221
Recycled radiators, kitchens and
bathrooms

Salvo Antique and Reclaimed
Materials for Buildings and Gardens
Ford Wood House
Berwick upon Tweed
TD15 2QF

Save Waste and Prosper (SWAP)
PO Box 19
6-8 Great George Street
Leeds LS1 6TF
tel: 0113 243877
Consultancy on recycling, energy
saving and waste reduction

Tradstocks
Dunaverig
Thornhill
Stirling FK8 3QW
tel: 01786 850400
Selection of reclaimed natural stone

Wastewatch
Gresham House
24 Holborn Viaduct
London EC1A 2BN
tel: 0171 248 0242
Information on recycling and
reducing waste

Environmental/Conservation

Common Ground
41 Shelton Street
London WC2H 9HJ
tel: 0171 379 3109
Charity working to conserve nature,
landscapes and place with the help
of people in all walks of the arts

The Environmental Agency
Waterside Drive
Aytec West
Normandsbury
Bristol BS12 4UD
tel: 0645 333111
Advises on water purity, rivers,
streams and inshore waters

National Conservancy Council
Northminster House
Peterborough
PE1 1UA
Advises on wildlife protection and
local conservation issues

Permaculture Association
8 Hunters Moon
Dartington
Totnes
Devon TO9 61T

Women's Environmental Network
Aberdeen Studios
22 Highbury Grove
London N5 2EA
tel: 0171 354 8823
Campaigns on a range of
environmental issues of particular
significance to women. Produces a
series of briefing papers on issues
such as chlorine, sanitary protection,
packaging and pesticides. Also runs
an information line

Low-allergen

British Allergy Foundation
St Bartholomew's Hospital
London EC1A 7BE
SAE for leaflets on coping with
allergies in the home

The Healthy House
Cold Harbour
Ruscombe
Stroud
Glos GL6 6DA
tel: 01453 752216
fax: 01453 753533
Mail-order catalogue specializing in
products suitable for people
suffering from allergies and
environmental illnesses. Range
includes non-toxic paints, low-
allergen bedding, air purifiers,
humidifiers, water filters and SAD
light boxes

Kingsmead Carpets
Crumswick
Ayrshire KA18 1SH
tel: 01290 421511
range of low-allergen dust mite-
protected carpets

National Asthma Campaign
300 Upper Street
London N1 2KK
tel: 0171 354 3593
A charity researching asthma
control. Provides wide range of
literature on low-allergen materials,
equipment and techniques

National Asthma Helpline
tel: 01345 010203

Ethical consumer goods

Little Green Shop
16 Gardner Street
Brighton
East Sussex BN1 IUP
tel: 01273 571221
Sells environmentally friendly
household products. Retail and mail
order

Natural paints, varnishes, stains

Auro Organic Paint Supplies Ltd
Unit 1
Goldstones Farm
Ashdon
Saffron Waldon
Essex TB1 2LZ

The Nature Made Co
Unit D7
Mawscraft Centre
Jackfield
Ironbridge TF8 7LS

Ostermann & Scheiwe UK Ltd
Osmo House
26 Swakeleys Drive
Ickenham
Middlesex UB10 8QD
tel: 01895 234 899

Green computer peripherals

Nighthawk Electronic Ltd
Freepost
Saffron Waldron
Essex CB11 3BR
tel: 01799 540881
fax: 01799 541713

Natural floorings:

The Alternative Flooring Company
14 Anton Trading Estate
Andover
Hants SP10 2NK
tel: 0500 007057

Crucial Trading
Showroom: 79 Westbourne
Park Road
London W2
tel: 0171 221 9000

Fired Earth
Twyford Mill
Oxford Road
Adderbury
Oxon OX17 3HP
tel: 01295 812088

Oxfam
272 Banbury Rad
Oxford OX2 7DZ

Traidcraft
Kingsway
Gateshead
Tyne & Wear
NE11 ONE

Waveney Rush Industry
Aldeby
Beccles
Suffolk NR34 0BL
tel: 01502 677345

Household cleaners

Ecover products
Full Moon
Charlton Court Farm
Mouse Lane
Steyning
West Sussex BN4 3DF
and various stores

Henry Flack
PO Box 78
Beckenham
Kent BR3 4BL
beeswax polish

Clean air and light

John Bell and Croydon
50 Wigmore Street
London W1
tel: 0171 937 5555
Health products inc. ionizers,
portable air conditioners, SAD light
boxes

London Ionizer Centre
65 Endell Street
London WC2H 9AJ

Mountain Breeze
Peel House
Peel Road
Skelmersdale
Lancs WN8 9PT

National Society for Clean Air
136 North Street
Brighton BN1 1RG
tel: 01273 326313

Organic plants, herbs and gardens

Henry Doubleday Research
Association (HDRA)
National Centre for Organic
Gardening
Ryton-on-Dunsmore
Coventry CV8 3LG
tel: 01203 303517
Membership includes newsletter and
free organic gardening advice

Soil Association
Bristol House
40-56 Victoria Street
Bristol BS1 6BY
email: soilassoc@gn.apc.org

The Soil Association (Organic Food
and Farming Centre)
86 Colston Street
Bristol BS1 5BB
tel: 0117 9290661
Leading UK organization for organic
farming; gives advice to consumers
on obtaining organic foods from
local farms plus extensive list of
publications and books

Suffolk Herbs
Monk Farm
Pantlings Lane
Kelvedon
Essex CO5 9PJ
tel: 01376 572456
Seed company, mail-order catalogue
with wide selection

Ethical consumer advice sources

The Building Bookshop
26 Store Street
London WC1E 7BT
tel: 0171 637 3151
Reference material and
manufacturers' literature

Department of the Environment
PO Box 151
London E15 2HF
fax: 0181 533 1618 for various
publications including: *Bothered by
Noise? What you can do about it?*, *Good
Air Quality in Your Home*

Ethical Consumer Research
Association
Unit 21
41 Old Birley Street
Manchester
M15 5RF

Ethical Investment Research &
Information Service (EIRIS)
Bondway Business Centre
71 Bondway
London SW8 1SQ

Ethical Consumer Magazine
published by ECRA Publishing Ltd
Unit 21, 41 Old Birley Street
Manchester M15 5RF
tel: 0161 226 2929
fax: 0161 226 6277
e-mail: ethicon@mcr1.poptel.org.uk

Friends of the Earth
26-28 Underwood Street
London N1 7JQ
tel: 0171 490 1555
Campaigns on various issues from
recycling, pesticides, transport
through to nuclear power.
Publications available

Electronic networking

An increasing amount of information
on green issues is available through
electronic and Internet networks.
Many environmentalists rely on fast,
cheap electronic communication to
stay in touch with colleagues around
the world.

GreenNet
4th Floor
393-395 City Road
London ECIV 1NE
tel: 0171 713 1941
fax: 0171 833 1169
email: support@gn.apc.org
Part of an international network
linking environmental, peace and
social justice groups

EnviroWeb
http://www.envirolink.org
Large on-line environmental
information service. Includes
environmental links, forums,
libraries, databases and green-
friendly cybermail

One World
http:/www.oneworld.org
Umbrella for 60-plus non-
governmental organizations and
charities

INDEX

ACKNOWLEDGEMENTS

The publishers would like to thank the following for the use of pictures:

Abode Interiors Photography & Library: pp 16, 17(b), 28(br), 33(ab), 34(ab), 35, 40(t), 42(t), 42(m), 46(bl), 48(m), 50/51, 51, 60(t), 64, 66(tl), 66(ml), 66/67, 67(b), 71, 80(bl), 80/81, 94/95, 96(bl), 99(tl), 101(t), 101(b), 102(t), 103(t), 104, 105(t), 106(bl), 107(bl), 116(t), 118(tr), 136(t)

AKG London: p 68(t)

Arcaid/Richard Bryant: pp 8, 13
Arcaid/Scott Frances: p181
Arcaid/Steve Lyman: p 111(tr)
Arcaid/Alberto Piovano: p 9(ab)
Arcaid/Petrina Tinslay/Belle: p12
Arcaid/Richard Waite: p 8
Arcaid/Rodney Weidland/Belle: pp 11(b),171(t)

Concord Lighting Limited: p 69

John Cullen Lighting: p 75(bl)

Creation Baumann: p 109(t)

Elizabeth Whiting Associates: pp18, 19, 20(m), 20(b), 21, 24/25, 28(tl), 33(m), 34(b), 38(tl), 38(ml), 38(bl), 38(br), 40(m), 44, 46/47, 47, 48(b), 54/55, 55, 56/57, 58, 59, 60(bl)(br), 61(bl), 66(bl), 67(t), 76/77, 79(mr), 86(ml), 89(tr), 93, 97, 98(b), 95(br), 99(mr), 102(b) 111(tl), 112/113, 116(m),116(b), 122, 123(l), 124(tl), 132/133, 136(b), 137(t), 143(m)(br), 145(b) 150(t), 168, 170, 171(b), 172(b),180

Garden Picture Library: pp 9(b), 118(bl), 119(tr), 123(r), 138(t)(m)(b), 139(t)(m), 143(tl), 144(tl)(bl), 144/145, 146, 147(br), 149, 150(b), 154(t)(m)(b), 155, 158/9, 179

Walter Gardiner Photography: p 28

Gleneagles: p 90(br)

Harlequin fabrics & wallcoverings: p 109(b)

Heron Parigi: p 52

Houses & Interiors/Rodger Brooks: pp 15, 50
Houses & Interiors/Simon Butcher: pp 17(ab), 38(ml), 108(r), 126(bl)
Houses & Interiors/Mark Bolton: pp 46(br), 61(br), 124(b)
Houses & Interiors/Gwenan Murphy: p 139(bl)

The Hutchison Library: p 115,181

The Image Bank: pp 20(tl), 45, 48(t), 78(ml), 80(tl), 82(tr), (mr),(b)(bl), 83,84(t),(b), 84/85, 91(bl), 96(tl)(tr), 108(l), 110(t), 110(b), 111(bl), 114/115, 120, 151, 152, 152/153, 153(m)(br)

Laura Ashley: pp 92(l), 107(t)

Netsurfer Ltd: p 53

Courtesy of Pioneer: p 121

The Stock Market Photo Agency: pp 6/7, 11(ab),14, 21, 90(l), 96/97, 98(tr), 99(br)

The publishers would like to thank the following for help with photography:

C & H Fabrics Ltd, Brighton; Luggage Plus, Lewes; Robert Hoare (Pine Antiques), Lewes